oñana National Park On...
the most important natur... ...British enclave on the Spanish
abitats in Spain *(page 61)* coast *(page 42)*

Ronda Its ancient bullring is the birthplace of the modern bullfight *(page 56)*

hite Towns With their whitewashed houses and winding reets, these are a major feature of Andalucía *(page 56)*

andy beaches The Costa del Sol is blessed with miles and iles of them

The Mezquita The magnificent Córdoban mosque was once the largest in the western Islamic world *(page 66)*

CONTENTS

50

82

17

INTRODUCTION

For thousands of years, the people of the Costa del Sol, except when invaded or in times of war, went about their business oblivious to the concerns of the outside world. But in the last half of the 20th century that changed dramatically when the Costa transformed itself from a collection of sleepy towns and fishing villages into the playground of the Western world.

Strung along the southern coast of Spain between Gibraltar in the southwest and Almería to the east, this Mediterranean coastline encompasses parts of Cádiz, Málaga, Granada and Almería – four of the eight provinces of Andalucía, Spain's southernmost autonomous community. The other provinces are Huelva, adjoining Portugal and the Atlantic Ocean, and landlocked Sevilla, Córdoba and Jaén. Surprisingly, the beaches on the Costa del Sol are not wide, with miles of yellow sand, as on the Atlantic coast. Rather, never far from the mountains and in some sections directly next to them, they are usually composed of a dull grey sand that has been formed by the erosion of these same mountains.

So what attracts millions of visitors from numerous countries every year? Well, for a start, bountiful sunshine almost all year round: the Costa del Sol has an average of 320 cloud-free days a year. Because the region is protected by an almost endless wall of mountains – the Sierra Nevada to the east of Málaga and the Serranía de Ronda to the west – it is spared the harsh, arid heat of the inland plateau. Temperatures in the summer rarely rise above 35°C (95°F). In addition, such a climate encourages an easygoing atmosphere; the local people still retain a gregarious, garrulous and generous nature, and tourists are made to feel very welcome here.

Hibiscus in Frigiliana, north of Nerja

West to Tarifa

Málaga's international airport is the primary gateway to the Costa del Sol, which can be subdivided into two sections, west and east of Málaga. The more familiar image of the Costa del Sol is to be found to the west, where development reaches far back from the beaches. In the original tourist boom town of Torremolinos, high-rise hotels and squat apartment blocks loom above the waterfront promenade and the bustling back streets are lined with pubs, clubs, discos, chip shops, curry houses and other amenities familiar to British tourists. The apartment complexes around the marina at Benalmádena, however, are far more attractive.

Marbella, though, is very different. The original play-ground of the 1960s jet set and the upmarket showcase of the Costa del Sol, it was first put on the map by Prince Alfonso von Hohenlohe in the 1950s. Today, movie stars, Arab potentates and other celebrities keep it in the news. In more

Málaga's Plaza de la Constitución

recent years, though, neighbouring Puerto Banús has emerged as the place to be seen. Magnificent yachts are moored in the marina, gourmet restaurants line the harbour, and sophisticated stores abound. Towards Estepona, hotels and apartment complexes diminish in number, as stretches of empty beach and green hillsides claim the landscape.

Traditional fishing boat

Continuing on, the familiar silhouette of the Rock of Gibraltar dominates the skyline. If you want to investigate further, it is accessible by the road that leads off the E15/N340 at San Roque and ends at La Linea de la Concepción, the border with Gibraltar. Across the bay, Algeciras is the gateway to North Africa, just across the Strait of Gibraltar. There are even better views from the *mirador* (viewpoint) on the hill as the road winds around to Tarifa, the western end of the Costa del Sol.

East to Almería

The eastern part of the Costa, from Málaga to Almería, is quieter and less intensively developed. Rincón de la Victoria and Torrox are the first couple of resorts, but you will have to travel to Nerja, the largest resort on this stretch of coast, to find anything approaching those in the western section. Even here, the atmosphere is considerably quieter. Very soon, after the mountains begin to drop precipitously towards the sea, wonderful views can be had from the road, with family resorts like La Herradura and Almuñécar nestled in bays.

This stretch of the Costa del Sol, in the Provincia de Granada, is now known as the Costa Tropical. Motril sits in the middle of an unexpectedly lush green delta planted variously with avocados, citrus fruits, sugar cane, bananas and bamboo, and is guarded to the west by Salobreña and its Moorish castle. Motril to Adra is a conservation area; besides being by far the least built-up of any area on the whole Costa del Sol, it is scenically the most dramatic. Conversely, the route across the plain after leaving Adra is the dreariest along the whole coast. Fortunately, the mountains again meet the sea close to the town of Aguadulce, enlivening the last few kilometres into the city of Almería.

Just east of the city of Almería is the Cabo de Gata natural park, which has some of the most deserted beaches in Andalucía. Heading north from the park, Mojácar is the only resort of any size before the border with Murcia.

Andalucía's Attractions

The attributes that led to the initial development of the Costa del Sol remain its major attractions. Air travel to the Costa is inexpensive and easy, with a wide choice of scheduled and charter flights. It has good beaches and the sun can be relied upon to shine nine days out of 10. It is one of the liveliest and most cosmopolitan resort areas in the world, whose attractions attractions range from swimming in the sea to skiing in the sierras.

A graceful Mudéjar archway in the Real Alcázar, Sevilla

Visitors who investigate beyond the beaches will

Andalusian landscape surrounding the historic town of Antequera in the mountains north of Málaga

find a collection of picturesque whitewashed villages. Beyond the mountains are numerous ancient cities whose histories are known throughout the world. There's Sevilla, famed for its bullfights and flamenco; Córdoba, the first capital of Moorish Spain; and Granada, capital of the last Moorish kingdom on the Iberian peninsula and home of the magnificent Alhambra palace. This is also where you'll find Jerez de la Frontera, headquarters of the world's sherry trade; Ronda, with its stunning gorge and 18th-century bullring; and Cádiz, considered the oldest city in Spain. Numerous *pueblos blancos* (white villages) dot the landscape of the interior.

It is these Andalucían towns and cities, suggesting those quintessential images, that come to mind when Spain is mentioned – places that are steeped in history, with romantic palaces, flamenco dancers and a sun-drenched landscape.

A BRIEF HISTORY

The southern part of Spain is at a geographical crossroads: it is the gateway between the Mediterranean and the Atlantic, and the crossing point between Africa and Europe. The strategic importance of its location has given rise to a long and turbulent history.

The earliest evidence of human occupation is provided by the Paleolithic cave paintings, some 25,000 years old, in the Cueva de la Pileta near Ronda. Neolithic peoples arrived on the scene in the 4th millennium BC, leaving behind signs of early attempts at agriculture and fragments of their pottery. Tribes of Iberians from North Africa crossed over into Spain around 3000BC and initiated Spain's first experiments in architecture; Spain's oldest structure stands near Antequera, a dolmen burial chamber known as the Cueva de Romeral. After 900BC, wandering bands of Celts entered the peninsula from northern Europe and brought to the area their knowledge of bronze and iron work. As they moved further south, the Celts merged with the Iberians and began to build walled villages along the coast.

Traders and Colonisers

About the same time that this was taking place, the Phoenicians were already venturing across the Mediterranean from their homeland in present-day Lebanon. They reached Spain by about 1100BC, founding many trading settlements in the land they called *Span* or *Spania*. The first was Gades (modern Cádiz), followed by Malaka (now Málaga) and Abdera (Adra) on the Costa del Sol. Contact with the sophisticated Phoenicians introduced the Celtiberians to the concept of currency.

After 650BC, Greek traders entered the competition to exploit Spain's rich mineral deposits and fertile land. Their influence was short-lived, although the olive and the grape, both Greek legacies, soon became important crops.

The Carthaginians, a North African people related to the Phoenicians, subsequently took over much of southern Spain, beginning with Cádiz in 501BC. They extended their influence along the River Guadalquivir to Sevilla, then to Córdoba. On the coast, they founded the city of Carteya, overlooking the Bay of Algeciras (240BC). Carthage, challenged by Rome in the First Punic War (264–241), lost most of its Spanish possessions to Iberian attacks. However, its fortunes changed with an initial victory in the Second Punic War (218–201).

Emboldened, the Carthaginian general Hannibal decided to advance on Rome. He led one of history's great military marches from Spain into Italy, crossing the Pyrenees and the Alps on the way. The Romans invaded Spain to cut off Hannibal's supply route – and stayed there for some 600 years.

The Roman Bridge in Córdoba

Roman Rule

It took the Romans two centuries to subdue the Iberians, but in the end most of the peninsula was incorporated into their new colony of Hispania. The south formed part of the province of Baetica, virtually identical to today's Andalucía, with Córdoba its capital.

The Romans had a far-reaching influence on the country. A road network was constructed (the Via Augusta ran the length of the south coast on its way to Rome) and bridges, aqueducts, villas and public buildings were added to the list of their achievements. The introduction of the Latin language (from which modern Spanish developed), Roman law (the basis of Spain's legal system) and, eventually, Christianity all brought about stability and a degree of unity.

Ultimately the Roman Empire began to crumble and the Romans withdrew from Spain. This left the country to be

Málaga's Alcazaba is a fortified palace built by the Moors

overrun by various barbarian tribes, especially the Vandals. The Visigoths, who controlled much of southern Spain for some 300 years, eventually dominated these tribes, but ultimately the Visigothic kingdom proved unstable. The monarchy was elective, rather than hereditary, which led to disputes over succession. During one of these altercations, the disaffected party looked to North Africa for an ally.

Moors and Christians

In AD711, some 12,000 Berber troops landed at Gibraltar, beginning a period of Moorish rule that was not finally broken by the Christians until nearly 800 years later. Following their victory at the Battle of Guadalete, the Moors (the name given to the Muslims in Spain) carried all before them. They pushed the Visigoths into the northern mountains and within 10 years most of the country had fallen to Islam.

The Moors chose Córdoba as their seat of government and from the 8th to the very early 11th century, it ranked as one of the great cities of the world. It was capital of the independent caliphate of Córdoba, founded by Abd-ar-Rahman III in 929. Under the caliphs, southern Spain knew prosperity and peace, for the Moors were relatively tolerant rulers and taxed non-believers rather than trying to convert them. Intellectual life flourished and great advances were made in science and medicine.

With the introduction of a sophisticated irrigation system, crops such as rice, cotton and sugar cane were cultivated for the first time on Spanish soil, as were or-

Moorish origins

To this day, Almuñécar, Tarifa, Algeciras, Benalmádena and several other towns are known by their Arabic names. All place names beginning with the prefix Al- have Moorish origins. Almería's Arabic name, for instance, means 'the mirror of the sea'.

anges, peaches and pomegranates. The manufacture of paper and glass were other Moorish innovations. Skilled engineers and architects, the Moors built numerous palaces and fortifications. As superb craftsmen they excelled in the production of ceramics and tooled leather, as well as delicate silverware.

The ensuing fall of Córdoba was as remarkable as its rise. In 1009, the caliphate splintered into a number of small kingdoms called *taifas*, which were constantly at war. The Christians in the north, seeing the enemy weakened and divided, captured the *taifa* of Toledo. Under threat of attack, the other *taifas* sought help from the Almoravids, fanatical Berber warriors. The Berbers marched against the Christians in 1086 and went on to reduce Moorish Spain to a province of their own North African Empire.

For a time the affairs of Muslim Spain were administered from the Almoravid headquarters in Granada, until the Almoravids, softened by a life of ease in Andalucía, lost their grip on the peninsula. The pattern repeated itself a century later when the Moors invoked the aid of the Almohads, from the Atlas Mountains of Morocco, in 1151. They soon made themselves the masters of southern Spain and constructed major fortifications, such as Sevilla's Alcázar, endowing the Moors with sufficient strength to resist the Christian forces a while longer.

Sevilla's Alcázar, a masterpiece of Moorish architecture

The fortunes of the Moors and Christians swayed back and forth until 1212, when the Christians gained their first decisive victory at Las Navas de Tolosa in northern Andalucía. The Christians gradually captured and annexed the former bastions of Moorish rule; in 1236, Córdoba fell to Jaime the Conqueror, followed by Sevilla in 1248. The Moors were in retreat, retrenching along the coast and withdrawing to the security of their strongholds in Ronda and Granada.

In military disarray and political decline, Moorish Spain nevertheless saw another two centuries of brilliance under the Nasrid dynasty, founded in Granada by Mohammed I in 1232. Refugees from Córdoba and

The Alhambra in Granada: the finest memorial to the Nasrids

Sevilla flooded into the city, bringing with them their talents and skills and adding to the city's brilliance. The magnificent palace of the Alhambra provided the setting for a luxurious court life dedicated to the pursuit of literature, music and the arts.

Yet the Moorish fortresses along the coast soon came under attack. Sancho IV took Gibraltar in 1310, but the Christians later relinquished their prize and the Moors held on to it until 1462. In the 1480s the Christians launched a new offensive; Ronda capitulated to the sovereigns Fernando and Isabela in 1485, followed by Málaga in 1487 and Almería in 1488. Granada was finally conquered in 1492.

The Golden Age

With the triumph of Christianity, the country was united under the Catholic Monarchs *(Los Reyes Católicos)*, a title conferred by Pope Alexander VI on Fernando II of Aragón and Isabela I of Castilla. Also in 1492, Cristobal Colón (Christopher Columbus) discovered the New World in the name of the Spanish crown. Fanatical in their religious zeal, the king and queen expelled all Jews who refused to convert to Christianity in the same year, followed by the Moors in 1502. The rulers thus reneged on the promise of religious freedom they had given when Granada surrendered. With the Jews who left Spain went many of the country's bankers and merchants, and with the Moors, a good number of its agriculturists and labourers. The converted Jews *(Conversos)* and Moors *(Moriscos)* who remained in Spain were viewed with suspicion by the Inquisition, which had been established by the Catholic Monarchs to suppress heresy. Many fled; many that couldn't were condemned to death.

Sevilla's Giralda: from mosque to bell tower

The 16th century was glorious for Spain, with the conquest of the New World bringing much prestige and wealth. In 1503, the Casa de Contratación in Sevilla was awarded a monopoly on trade with Spain's territories in the Americas. For more than two centuries, Sevilla was the richest city in Spain.

By comparison, coastal settlements languished and were subject to frequent raids by Barbary pirates. Under constant threat for more than 200 years, the population drifted inland, taking refuge in fortified towns and villages hidden in the foothills of the sierras.

Tomb of Fernando and Isabela in the Capilla Real, Granada

Emperor Carlos V of the Holy Roman Empire, the first Habsburg Spanish king, turned his attention to European events. Between 1521 and 1556, he went to war with France four times, squandering the riches of the Americas on endless military campaigns. Carlos also had a weakness for such costly projects as his vast Renaissance palace in the grounds of the Alhambra, which he commissioned in 1526. Taxes imposed on the Moors served to finance the building works, which eventually had to be abandoned for lack of funds when the Moriscos revolted 12 years into the reign of Felipe II (1556–98). The king dispatched his half-brother, Don Juan of Austria, to quell the rebellion, which ended in 1570 with the defeat of the Moriscos and their eventual dispersal. In 1588, Felipe II prepared to invade England, only to be repulsed when the English navy destroyed Spain's previously invincible Armada.

The defeat marked the start of a long decline. Felipe's military forays and his expensive tastes left Spain encumbered with debts. Participation in the Thirty Years' War under Felipe III led to further financial difficulties and to another debacle in 1643, when Spanish troops were defeated by the French at Rocroi in Flanders, never to regain their prestige.

French Ascendancy

Spain's internal affairs became the concern of the other great powers after Carlos II died without an heir. The Habsburg Archduke Charles of Austria challenged the French Philip of Bourbon in the ensuing War of the Spanish Succession. Gibraltar was the scene of some fierce fighting in 1704, when Britain captured the Rock on behalf of Austria. Under the terms of the Treaty of Utrecht, which also confirmed Philip's right to the Spanish throne, Spain was finally forced to relinquish its claims to Gibraltar in 1713.

Nearly 100 years later, during the Napoleonic Wars, Spanish ships fought alongside the French fleet against Lord Nelson at Cape Trafalgar *(see below)*. But as the wars continued, Napoleon, distrustful of his ally, forced the Spanish king Fernando VII to abdicate in 1808 and imposed his own brother, Joseph, as king. He then sent thousands of troops across the Pyrenees to subjugate the Spanish, who promptly revolted. Aided by British troops, who were subsequently commanded by the Duke of Wellington, the Spanish drove the French from the Iberian Peninsula. At Tarifa, the enemy was defeated literally overnight in an offensive of 1811. What the English-speaking world knows as the Peninsular War

The Battle of Trafalgar

Fifty kilometres (30 miles) northwest of Tarifa lies the Cabo de Trafalgar (from the Arabic *Tarif al-Gar*, or Cape of the Cave). Off this headland on 21 October 1805, a British fleet of 27 ships under Admiral Horatio Nelson engaged 33 French and Spanish vessels in one of history's most famous naval battles, which established Britain's naval supremacy for the next 100 years. The enemy was routed, losing nearly two-thirds of its ships. No British vessels were lost, but Nelson was hit by a sniper's bullet and died just before the battle's end.

(1808–14) is referred to in Spain as the War of Independence. During this troubled period, Spain's first, short-lived, constitution was drafted and Spanish colonies in South America won their independence.

Troubled Times

Fernando's return to the throne in 1814 destroyed any hopes left for a constitutional monarchy, but tension between liberals and conservatives led to a century of conflict, marked by the upheavals of the three Carlist wars.

When Fernando died in 1833 his three-year-old daughter María Cristina Isabela was proclaimed queen. Her right to succeed was disputed by supporters of her uncle, Don Carlos, and her succession precipitated the first Carlist war (1833–9).

Ramón Narváez is commemorated in his home town of Loja

While Isabela was a child, first her mother then General Baldomero Espartero acted as regents, but in 1843 Espartero was deposed by military officers and Isabela, still only 13, was declared queen in her own right. Her reign, which lasted until 1868, was characterised by political unrest and a series of uprisings. Her government was dominated by military politicians, notably General Ramón María Narváez, Prime Minister several times, and the somewhat more liberal General Leopoldo O'Donnell. Liberal opposition to the regime's authoritarianism became increasingly directed at Isabela. Scandalous reports on the private conduct of the queen, who lived apart from her husband, Francisco de Asís de Borbón, as well as her arbitrary political interference, further damaged the monarchy's cause. An abortive uprising in 1866, and the deaths of O'Donnell and Narváez soon afterwards, weakened her position further. In the autumn of 1868 a successful revolution drove her into exile.

Isabela settled in Paris, where in 1870 she abdicated in favour of her eldest surviving son, Alfonso. After a short-lived First Republic, proclaimed in 1873, Alfonso ascended the throne in 1874 and monarchy returned to Spain for another 50 years.

On the Andalucían coast, the 19th century was a time of tentative expansion. With piracy at an end, a number of towns and villages grew up along the shoreline and the extension of the railway line to Almería in 1899 promoted the early development of the eastern region.

The Second Republic

Alfonso XIII, just 16 years old, assumed the crown in 1902. Prosperity and stability continued to elude the country, which remained neutral during World War I. Against a murky background of violence, strikes and regional strife, the king accepted the dictatorship of General Miguel Primo de Rivera in 1923. Seven years later, the opposition of radical forces toppled Primo de Rivera from power. King Alfonso went into exile following anti-royalist election results in 1931 and another republic was founded.

The parliamentary elections of 1933 produced a swing to the right and public opinion in Spain became polarised. When the left came out on top in the elections of 1936, the situation began to deteriorate at an alarming rate. Six months later, General Francisco Franco led a large section of the army against the elected government. Support for the Franco-led nationalist uprising came from monarchists, conservatives and the right-wing Falangist organisation, as well as the Roman Catholic Church, while liberals, socialists, communists and anarchists sided with the government.

The bloodshed of the Spanish Civil War lasted for three years and cost hundreds of thousands of lives. Franco emerged as the leader of a shattered Spain. Many republicans went into exile; others simply disappeared. (The republican mayor of Mijas caused a sensation when he surfaced in the 1960s after three decades in hiding – in his own home.) Franco kept the impoverished country out of World War II, despite Hitler's entreaties. The Spanish nation gradually managed to heal its wounds, although conditions were extremely difficult for many years and life was a struggle for many people.

Italian planes bomb the republicans in the Civil War

Changing Fortunes

All that was to change when Spain's tourist potential began to be exploited in the late 1950s. Spain's admission to the United Nations in 1955, followed by the advent of jet travel and package holidays in the 1960s, subsequently opened up the coast to mass tourism.

With the death of Franco in 1975, Spain became a democracy. The monarchy was restored in the person of King Juan Carlos, the grandson of Alfonso XIII. More than just a figurehead, the king helped to thwart a military coup in 1981, keeping Spain firmly on a democratic course. A process of decentralisation was begun, with powers being devolved to 17 semi-autonomous regions and on 28 February 1982, Andalucía was given autonomous status.

The border with Gibraltar was reopened in February 1985, after a 16-year hiatus, and Spain joined the EC in 1986. In 1992 Sevilla hosted Expo '92, and investment poured into Andalucía.

A terrorist attack on Madrid's commuter trains dominated the 2004 election won by the Socialist party under José Luis Rodriguez Zapatero, who became prime minister. In 2006, several members of Marbella town council were arrested in a corruption scandal based around granting planning permission in return for gifts and favours. The credit crunch of 2008–9 hit Andalucía particularly hard, bringing to an end a building boom that had gone on almost non-stop for forty years and compounding the region's problem of high unemployment. Other current political issues include immigration from Eastern European countries, Africa and South America and the best way to save what is left of the Costa del Sol's fragile natural environment.

Juan Carlos became king after Franco's death in 1975

Historical Landmarks

circa **3000BC** Iberian tribes migrate to Spain from North Africa.

1100BC Phoenicians found coastal settlements.

900BC Celts migrate south from northern Europe.

650BC Greek traders found a series of colonies.

2nd century BC Romans conquer Spain.

5th century AD Visigothic kingdom established.

711 Moors launch their conquest of Spain.

929 Caliphate of Córdoba founded.

11th–12th century The caliphate splinters into small kingdoms called *taifas*.

1212 Christians defeat Moors at Las Navas de Tolosa.

1232 Nasrid dynasty founded in Granada.

1492 Granada falls to Fernando and Isabela. Cristobal Colón discovers America.

16th century Emperor Carlos V and King Felipe II expand Spain's empire during the Golden Age.

1609 The Moors are finally expelled from Spain.

1704 Great Britain captures Gibraltar.

1808 Napoleon sets his brother, Joseph, on the Spanish throne, triggering the War of Independence (1808–14).

1873 Proclamation of Spain's first (short-lived) republic.

1902–31 Political unrest grows under King Alfonso XIII.

1931-6 Second Republic.

1936–39 Spanish Civil War: at least 600,000 die.

1939–75 Dictatorship of General Francisco Franco.

1975 Spain becomes a constitutional monarchy.

1982 Andalucía is given autonomous status.

1986 Spain enters European Union (then the EC).

1992 Sevilla hosts Expo '92. High-speed train link (the AVE) established, cutting journey time to Madrid to two hours.

2002 The euro replaces the peseta as the currency of Spain.

2004 Bomb attacks on Madrid commuter trains. Socialists elected

2006 Corruption scandal erupts in Marbella.

WHERE TO GO

Most visitors to the Costa del Sol are based in one of the large coastal resorts to the west of Málaga (Torremolinos, Benalmádena, Fuengirola, Marbella or Estepona), while far fewer head east towards Nerja, Almuñécar, or even as far as Almería. Although the main aim for many is to relax on the beach and soak up as much sun as possible, increasing numbers arrive to play golf. It comes as little surprise, therefore, that the road signs proclaim the area west of Málaga not just as the *Costa del Sol*, but also the *Costa del Golf*.

A few visitors forsake the beach for a day or two and venture out to the amazingly varied historic towns and cities or to the natural wonders of the national parks nearby. Málaga, Ronda, Gibraltar, Sevilla, Córdoba, Granada or the national parks can be visited on a day or overnight trip depending on where you are based.

MÁLAGA

Málaga's international airport is the gateway to the Costa del Sol and Andalucía for most people. However, few visitors spend much time in the city itself. This is a shame, because Málaga is an ancient Andalucían city of considerable charm that offers a refreshing taste of the real Spain.

Founded by Phoenician traders more than 3,000 years ago, it came under Carthaginian and Roman rule before falling to the Moorish invasion force in 711. The Moors fortified the city, developing the settlement into a major trading port serving Granada, and it was one of the last cities in Spain to be reconquered by Christian forces in 1487.

The famous cathedral in Sevilla is Europe's third-largest church

A good place to begin a tour is at Málaga's principal landmark, the **Castillo del Gibralfaro** (from the Arabic *Jebel al Faro* – Lighthouse Hill). Located some 130m (425ft) above the city, this hill is capped by the ramparts of a Phoenician castle reconstructed in the 14th century by the Moors, who went on to build the lighthouse that gave Gibralfaro its name. The walls and parapets offer a superb panoramic view of both the city below and the coastline disappearing into the horizon. Because it looks down on the Plaza de Toros, the hill also acts as free seating for bullfight enthusiasts.

It is possible to walk up here but it is not recommended as it's a steep climb and the path can be a hangout for muggers. It's best to take a taxi or a bus from the delightful **Paseo del Parque**, with contrasting fountains at either end, which connects the old town with the Plaza de Toros. On its south side, it is a lush seaside tropical garden enhanced by fountains, duck ponds and small bars. The other side is home to the smaller Jardínes Puerta Oscura and two impressive buildings, the Ayuntamiento (Town Hall) and the 18th-century La Aduana (Old Custom House).

Immediately behind is the **Alcazaba**, a fortified palace complex built by the Moors in the 8th century. A cobbled path climbs up the hillside within the walls to the Arco del Cristo (Gateway of Christ). The victorious Christian army of Fernando and Isabela celebrated Mass here when the fortress finally fell into their hands in 1487. Higher still, the palace itself contains a small archaeological museum. Beside the entrance to the Alcazaba are

La Manquita

Málaga's vast cathedral is known locally as La Manquita – the one-armed lady – because only one of its twin towers was completed. The north tower soars 100m (330ft) above the street, but work on the other, a forlorn stump of stone, stopped in 1783 because of a lack of money.

A bird's eye view of the bullring from the Castillo del Gibralfaro

the excavated ruins of the 2nd-century **Teatro Romano**, the only visible remains of the Roman city.

Málaga was the birthplace, in 1881, of Pablo Ruiz Picasso, although the artist left his native city at the age of 14 for Madrid and Barcelona. The house where he was born, **Casa Natal Picasso** (Mon–Sat 9.30am–8pm; charge; www.fundacion picasso.es) at Plaza de la Merced 14, is a small museum and headquarters of the Picasso Foundation. On a much grander scale, the **Museo Picasso** (Tue–Thur, Sun and holidays 10am–8pm, Fri–Sat 10am–9pm; charge; www.museopicasso malaga.org) is housed in the impressive Palacio de Buenavista, which dates from 1542. As well as displaying about 200 of Picasso's works, the museum highlights the history of the city.

The **Museo Unicaja de Artes Populares** (Mon–Fri 10am–1.30pm, 5–8pm, 4–6pm in winter, Sat 10am–1.30pm; charge; www.museoartespopulares.com) on the western edge

Fresh local produce in
the Mercado Atarazanas

of the old town, offers a fascinating glimpse into how life was lived in Málaga in generations past.

On the way back to the centre of Málaga, stop for a moment or two at the neo-Mudéjar building housing the **Mercado Atarazanas** (market). Each morning it is filled with women admiring the bountiful displays of meat, fish, fruit and vegetables, and shopping for fresh, not plastic-wrapped, produce. This is also the western boundary of a collection of small roads and pedestrianised streets that end at the main street, Calle Marqués de Larios (now pedestrianised itself), and combine to form Málaga's principal shopping centre. You can buy almost anything here, from foodstuffs to footwear, but remember that the siesta still reigns in this part of Spain and nothing is open in the afternoon between about 2pm and 5pm.

WEST OF MÁLAGA

Some of Europe's most popular beach resorts line the coast that stretches 160km (100 miles) to the Rock of Gibraltar.

Torremolinos

Just a few kilometres west of Málaga's international airport lies **Torremolinos**. In the late 1950s and early 1960s, it was the first resort on the Costa del Sol to establish a reputation as a popular international playground. Although little more than an overgrown village, it was a haven for young northern

Europeans seeking an inexpensive holiday with sun, sand and sangría. Since then, it has built, quite literally, on that reputation, and has long been a highly popular tourist destination, with accommodation tens of thousands of visitors – much of it in high-rise blocks. Wall-to-wall hotels and apartments reach back in rows from the beaches and there's no denying that it delivers everything sun-hungry visitors could wish for. Miles of glorious beaches, cheap alcohol and familiar food, numerous bars, discos and nightclubs attract a clientele that is largely British, although Germans, Scandinavians and others also arrive in large numbers. This international invasion has completely overwhelmed the town and foreign languages are more dominant than Spanish.

Although the first mention of Torremolinos dates back to 1498, there is really nothing here of historical significance. The town itself, especially **Calle San Miguel**, is simply a profusion of shops. At the bottom of San Miguel a series of winding stairways leads down towards a 7-km (4-mile) sweep of golden coastline. This consists of six **beaches** connected by the Paseo Marítimo (beach promenade) and broken only by the rocky promontory of Castillo de Santa Clara, which separates the Bajondillo (east) and Carihuela (west) sections of town.

Downtown Torremolinos

High-rise hotels line the Torremolinos beaches

Chiringuitos (small beachside restaurants) are in plentiful supply, especially in the former fishing village of **La Carihuela**. There are still a few bona-fide fishermen about and if you drag yourself out of bed between 6am and 8am, you'll see them returning in their gaily painted, flat-bottomed wooden boats, with nets of sardines and anchovies. At lunchtime, you can sample the morning's catch, skewered on a wooden stick and grilled over a fire on the beach.

Many other popular attractions lie close at hand, including the wave pools and water slides of **Aqualand** and the 18-hole course of the nearby Parador del Golf. But the biggest draw in Torremolinos are the bars and clubs that have earned the resort its reputation for noisy, non-stop nightlife.

Benalmádena-Costa

Heading west it appears, at first glance, that Benalmádena-Costa is indistinguishable from its close neighbour, but this isn't really so. It is somewhat less built up and frenetic than Torremolinos, even though it's well endowed with bars, discos and clubs. Its fine beaches stretch for 9km (5 miles), beginning at the large and attractive Puerto Deportivo on the border with Torremolinos. Focal points are the three Moorish watchtowers; the pink, mock-Moorish walls of **Castillo de Bil-Bil**, built by a Frenchwoman in the 1930s and used for concerts, exhibitions and as a tourist office; and one of the Costa del Sol's casinos in the huge and impressive Torrequebrada complex.

Two kilometres (1 mile) inland and high above the sea lies the pretty, whitewashed village of **Benalmádena**. Its **Museo Arqueológico de Benalmádena** (Tue–Sat 9.30am–1.30pm, 4–7pm, Sun 10am–2pm; charge) takes pride in a collection of pre-Columbian art, with jewellery, statuary and ceramics from Central America. Also in the Benalmádena area is the **Tívoli World** amusement park, in Arroyo de la Miel (see page 92), the **Sea Life** aquarium in the Puerto Deportivo and **Eagle Park** at the Castillo de Colomares.

Benalmádena Buddhism

High above the Costa del Sol near Benalmádena stands an extraordinarily conspicuous and incongruent religious monument, the **Enlightenment Stupa**. Europe's largest stupa (a sacred Buddhist monument) isn't easy to miss when you are driving past on the motorway because of its 33-m (108-ft) golden spire. It's worth visiting for two reasons: the location on a platform high above sea level from which there are expansive views over the coast; and the building itself which inside consists of a light and peaceful prayer hall presided over by a statue of the Buddha. The walls are decorated by paintings by Nepalese artists. The whole place radiates a refreshing sense of peace and makes a good place to take a moment out from the pace of life on the beaches below.

Fuengirola

Located 9km (6 miles) down the road, **Fuengirola** is another resort that's hugely popular with the British. Here bacon and eggs, fish and chips, darts, snooker, English beer and bars showing football matches on television are the norm. But Fuengirola has assimilated this without losing all its Spanish character. This is particularly true in early October, during the annual fair, when the town becomes a blaze of colour and noise and almost every man, woman and child dons typical Andalucían dress. Tradition survives, too, in the commercial fishing fleet, which is an ongoing concern.

The Plaza de la Constitución in the town centre has numerous pleasant cafés lining the square beneath the church bell tower, and nearby are the bullring and the small **Zoológico Municipal** (zoo; daily 10am–6pm).

Across the river at the western end of town rise the remains of the **Castillo de Sohail**. Abd-er-Rahman III built this hilltop fortress in the 10th century and gradually a settlement grew up around the walls. Taken by the Christians in a bloody battle in 1487, Sohail was then levelled on the orders of the Catholic Monarchs. After it was rebuilt, it was occupied during the Peninsular War by French troops who left behind the cannon that are now displayed along the promenade of the **Paseo Marítimo**. Today its rooms are used for cultural events. Other attractions here include a variety of water

Varied attractions

Selwo (www.selwo.es) has three different enterprises in Benalmádena.
The Selwo Marina has dolphin shows and a Penguinarium, while the Selwo Teleférico whisks you up to Monte Calamorro for great views, donkey rides and falconry shows. Further down the coast, the Selwo Aventura safari park has some 2,000 animals and also offers African-style accommodation.

On the beach in Fuengirola

sports, a marina, the fishing harbour, a sailing school, the waterslides of the **Mijas Aqua Park**, the El Cartujano horse show and horse racing at the Mijas Hippodrome.

Mijas

Clinging to the hillside 8km (5 miles) inland from Fuengirola is **Mijas**. Surrounded by modern villas and *urbanizaciones* (developments), it looks from the outside like any other quaint village with whitewashed houses. But Mijas is different. Most of the houses have been converted into upmarket shops, restaurants or bars, making the whole village a tourist attraction. Traffic is banned from the centre, so if you don't feel like the short walk from the car park, you will have to take a mule taxi.

Mijas has a lovely **bullring** and, opposite, beautifully tended gardens slope down to a cliff-top *mirador*, with fine views all along the coast. There is another viewpoint beside the car park. On one side of this natural balcony you will find a tiny **chapel** dedicated to La Virgen de la Peña, set in a grotto carved from living rock. The Virgin is celebrated in a lively festival in September.

Marbella and Puerto Banús

Sheltered by the mountains of the Sierra Blanca on one side and with the Mediterranean on the other, Marbella has earned a reputation for being the most aristocratic of Costa del Sol's resorts. This began in the 1950s when Prince Alfonso von Hohenlohe bought land and built himself a luxurious home here. It became so popular with his guests that he developed it into the Marbella Club Hotel and that in turn launched Marbella as a trendy gathering place for the jet set in the 1960s. Today the town is still a playground for the rich and famous, frequented by celebrities and politicians, royalty and business tycoons. As a consequence, it has promoted the further development, both here and along the coast, of the largest collection of luxury hotels in Spain.

A pretty corner in Marbella's old town

Marbella is a town in two distinct parts. The largest by far is the modern section and the centre of this, clustered around the palm trees and fountains of the Parque de la Alameda, is taken up with busy pavement cafés, smart boutiques, banks and estate agents' offices. It is at its most attractive, though, by the sea, where the municipality of Marbella encompasses some 28km (17 miles) of beachfront. The promenade winds along the beaches of El Fuerte and Fontanilla, passing Puerto Deportivo, a **marina** with moorings for several hundred pleasure boats, overlooked by the tall spire of the light-

The elegant Iglesia de la Encarnación in Marbella

house. Some lively beach bars and restaurants make this a popular part of town.

The promenade extends west for a mile or two, between attractive apartment complexes and long stretches of golden sands. The monuments of modern Marbella cling to the hills on the western outskirts. The King of Saudi Arabia's holiday home – it looks a bit like the White House in Washington DC, only slightly larger – hides behind a row of pines and palms on a hilltop just above the highway, surrounded by high security fences. On a neighbouring hill stands Marbella's modern-style mosque, the **Mezquita del Rey Abdulaziz Al Saud** (open every afternoon 5–7pm except Friday).

But Marbella has its historic side, too. In fact, its history goes back some 1,600 years, even though most of what can be seen, in the town at least, dates from the time of the Catholic Monarchs or later. North of the main road, the

➤ **Casco Antiguo** (Old Town) provides an intriguing glimpse of the past, cleverly integrated to cater to modern visitors. First, sit at a café table in the **Plaza de los Naranjos** (Square of the Orange Trees), where you can admire the noble 16th-century façade of the **Ayuntamiento** (Town Hall) and soak up the atmosphere. Then wander through the maze of narrow streets where the whitewashed walls are decorated with colourful baskets of flowers.

Bonsai collection

Visitors with a fascination for very small trees should visit Marbella's **Museo del Bonsai** (daily 10am–1.30pm, 5–8pm, 4–6.30pm in winter), the only one in Spain and one of the best in the world.

As you explore the neighbourhood, you'll come across the historic parish church with a landmark bell tower and the convents of La Trinidad and San Francisco (it is said that Miguel de Cervantes, creator of Don Quixote, lodged at the latter). Uphill from the church lie the crumbling walls of the Moorish *castillo*. Scattered throughout this area is an eclectic array of shops and galleries. The **Museo del Grabado Español Contemporáneo** (Museum of Contemporary Spanish Prints; winter Mon and Sat 9am–2pm, Tue–Fri 9am–9pm, 6–9pm, summer Mon and Sat 9am–2pm, Tue–Fri 9am–2pm and 6–9pm; charge), housed in the old Bazán Hospital, contains works by Picasso, Miró, Tapiés and other renowned artists.

Just outside Marbella are three other places with ancient historical connections: the **Roman Villa mosaics** dating from the 1st and 2nd centuries at Río Verde near the beach; the Paleo-Christian basilica, **Vega del Mar**, in San Pedro de Alcántara; and **Las Bovedas** (The Cellars), the ruins of Roman baths at Guadalmina.

With the increasing popularity of Marbella, high society has moved west to the chic suburb of Nueva Andalucía and its magnificent harbour, **Puerto Banús**. Sleek, unbelievably expensive yachts line the quayside, and Porsches, Rolls-Royces and Mercedes fill the streets. There's a glamorous line-up of expensive restaurants and high-class boutiques that seem to be permanently open. High rollers haunt the tables in the nearby Casino Marbella, then sip martinis and watch the sun rise from the decks of their luxury yachts. Even if you can't afford to join in, it's fun just to watch how the other half lives. If you prefer to watch fish, the aquarium in Puerto Banús is small, but nonetheless interesting.

This part of the Costa del Sol is also a golfer's paradise. There are 30 golf clubs in operation between Málaga and Sotogrande. These courses cater to all levels, from beginners to professionals. At least half a dozen quality courses can be found between the western edge of Marbella and San Pedro de Alcántara.

Puerto Banús provides moorings for seriously expensive yachts

Ojén

Inland from Marbella lie the high peaks of the Sierra Blanca, the most distinctive being La Concha (The Seashell), which rises directly above the town. A scenic road leads to the village of **Ojén** (famous for *aguardiente*, a fierce anise spirit produced here) and on to the mountain pass called Puerto de Ojén. Just beyond, a road on the left leads to the **Refugio de Juanar**, a hunting lodge set at the heart of a large national game reserve. The peace and tranquillity found here has attracted numerous personalities, among them General Charles de Gaulle of France, who finished his memoirs here in 1970.

Estepona

The last major resort town on the western part of the Costa del Sol, Estepona provides all the essentials for a good holiday – nice beaches, golf courses, restaurants and a marina – with a small-town atmosphere. Low-rise apartment blocks, simple restaurants and hotels overlook the attractive palm-lined promenade, the **Paseo Marítimo**.

Originally a Roman settlement, Estepona preserves the remains of Moorish fortifications, an 18th-century parish

Floral display in Estepona

church and an expressionistic bullring, a startling piece of modern architecture that is beginning to look rather the worse for wear. On either side of the town itself, gracious and upmarket hotels are beginning to make an impression on the coastline.

Beyond Estepona, development is more sporadic, although there are some luxury resorts at Sotogrande and

The rooftops of Casares

Puerto Duquesa. About 6km (4 miles) outside town, a mountain road takes you up to **Casares**, a spectacular white hilltop village clinging precariously to the rugged slopes below its Moorish fort. The road, lined with eucalyptus trees, commands sweeping views of the coast and countryside, and on a clear day the eye is inevitably drawn to the twin peaks known in ancient times as the Pillars of Hercules – the Rock of Gibraltar on the right and Morocco's Jebel Musa on the left.

Gibraltar looms ever larger as you approach **San Roque**, which was established by Spanish refugees who fled the Rock when the English captured it in 1704. Building blocks for the town were found, conveniently, in the nearby ruins of Roman Carteya (little remains today of the classical site). Branch off the main road here and head for **La Línea de la Concepción** and the Rock itself. La Línea has experienced a mini-boom since the border with Gibraltar was reopened in 1985 after a blockade lasting 16 years, but is still a dreary place.

The Rock of Gibraltar, once thought to be the edge of the world

Gibraltar

Gibraltar was a home for pre-historic man: neanderthal skulls were found in 1848 and 1928 and this is considered one of the final bastions for this species. Although it is known that the Phoenicians, Greeks and Carthaginians were aware of Gibraltar and that the Romans controlled the region from about 500BC to AD475, no town was ever built. The Visigoths and Vandals destroyed almost all traces of culture in the area and it wasn't until long after the Moors invaded, in 711, that the first city was constructed. However, even that wasn't completed until nearly 450 years later, in 1160.

The next three centuries saw numerous battles and it was not until 1462 that Gibraltar was finally reconquered by the Spanish. In the early 18th century, problems over succession to the Spanish throne led to an Anglo-Dutch force capturing Gibraltar in 1704. Under the Treaty of Utrecht in 1713 Spain ceded its rights to Gibraltar to the British – although not without a fight. In 1727, their first siege failed, as did the Great Siege (1779–83), when Spanish and French forces totalling 50,000 men attacked just 5,000 defenders. Despite nearly four years of hardship, the British refused to surrender. In 1830 Gibraltar achieved the status of a British Crown Colony, which it still holds.

The town and harbour lie on the east slope of the Rock, overlooking the bay, with the narrow defile of **Main Street** cutting through the middle. This is lined with duty-free shops selling alcohol, perfume, cameras and electronic goods, and English-style pubs serving pints of bitter. The currency is the Gibraltarian pound (equal to the British pound), but shops and other businesses accept both sterling and euros.

Also at sea level is the **Gibraltar Museum** (Mon–Fri 10am–6pm, Sat 10am–2pm), with what are considered to be the best-preserved Moorish baths in Europe. The museum has interesting exhibits on Gibraltar's history. Of interest, too, is **Nelson's Anchorage**, where Admiral Nelson's body is said to have been brought in a barrel of rum after the Battle of Trafalgar in October 1805, and the nearby 100-tonne Victorian super-gun, the largest of its type in the world.

Main Street ends at the Referendum Gates, and beyond lies the **cable-car station**, where you can take a trip to the top of the Rock, with a stop halfway to visit the **Apes' Den**. The so-called Barbary apes (actually tailless macaque monkeys) that inhabit the Rock are natives of North Africa, descended from animals brought over by sailors as pets and ships' mascots. Legend has it that if the apes ever leave the Rock, then British rule will come to an end. When the apes' population declined significantly during World War II, Winston Churchill was worried and the monkeys have been well cared for ever since. The views from the summit 426m (1,400ft) up are spectacular, particularly across the strait to

Gibraltar is the only place in Europe to see wild Barbary apes

Morocco, along the coast towards Estepona and down the sheer east face of the Rock to the water-holding areas (for desalination) and the beaches of Sandy Bay, Catalan Bay and Eastern Beach.

From the upper cable car station you can follow the paths around the **Upper Rock Nature Reserve** which has a dense Mediterranean scrub vegetation harbouring 530 kinds of plant, including some rare species, growing on the alkaline limestone soils. This area is good for birdwatching too, especially during the spring and summer migrations when Gibraltar marks the shortest route between Europe and Africa.

St Michael's Cave (daily 9.30am–6.15pm) is an impressive natural grotto containing stalagmites and stalactites that is sometimes used as a venue for musical performances. At the north end of the Rock are the **Great Siege Tunnels**, a system of galleries blasted through the inside of the rock face during the 18th-century Great Siege. Note that the cannon emplacements slope downwards, a clever innovation that allowed the defenders to fire directly at the Spanish and French forces attacking from La Línea. What cannot be seen is the 51km (32 miles) of tunnels excavated during World War II. It was from these that General Eisenhower conducted the Allied invasion of North Africa.

Algeciras

Just across the bay from Gibraltar is an uninspiring port town whose only saving grace, on good days at least, is its unsurpassed views of the Rock. From the harbour, hydrofoils and car ferries cross the strait to Ceuta, a Spanish protectorate in North Africa, and to Tangier in Morocco. A day trip to Ceuta is certainly possible, but there is not much of interest there, beyond shopping. Much more interesting and exciting is to continue on about 40km (25 miles) to **Tetuan** in Morocco, parts of which seem to have remained unchanged for centuries. Because of the two-hour time difference between Ceuta and Morocco, it's difficult, but possible, to see it in one day, so an overnight stop in Ceuta is recommended.

Tarifa

Tarifa is where the waters of the Mediterranean mingle with those of the Atlantic and bring the Costa del Sol to an end. Europe looks across the Strait of Gibraltar to Africa, with the Rif Mountains of Morocco dominating the horizon a mere 13km (8 miles) away. A section of the old Moorish walls remains, as does the 10th-century fortress.

However, it is not its history that attracts most visitors these days. The beaches stretching to the west are such a mecca for windsurfers and kitesurfers that Tarifa is often called the windsurf capital of Europe. The pre-

Picturesque alleyway in Tarifa

Tarifa's beaches stretching away to the west

vailing wind, known as the *poniente*, is from the west, making the beaches among the windiest in Europe.

The windsurfers are not the only ones to take advantage of the reliable breeze; the hillsides above the town have sprouted a forest of wind-powered electricity turbines. In spring and autumn, storks, buzzards and other soaring birds fill the skies as they climb in the rising thermals before gliding across the strait on their annual migration, congregating here where the sea crossing is at its shortest.

EAST OF MÁLAGA

The eastern part of the Costa del Sol stretches for over 200km (125 miles) from Málaga all the way to Almería. This part of the coast has a very different feel from the western section, with less intensive development and, in parts, a much rockier and more attractive shoreline.

Málaga to Nerja

Leaving Málaga's suburbs, you arrive immediately in **Rincón de la Victoria**, a resort given over to weekend apartments owned by Spanish city-dwellers. But prehistoric man was here first, occupying the **Cueva del Tesoro** (Treasure Cave; daily passes 10.45am, 11.30am, 12.15pm, 1pm, 3.45pm, 4.30pm and 5.15pm, longer hours in summer; charge) on the Málaga side of the town. Cave paintings and prehistoric remains have been discovered, and there is a beautiful underground lake with stalactites. According to legend, five Moorish kings buried some huge treasure inside the cave, but it has never been found.

Torre del Mar is the gateway to the wine region of the Axarquía, and its capital, **Vélez-Málaga**, which lies 4km (2½ miles) inland. Founded by the Phoenicians, Vélez sprawls around an historic centre dominated by a Moorish *alcazaba* (citadel) and two venerable churches: the late-Gothic Iglesia de San Juan Bautista and the Iglesia de Santa María (incorporating part of the town's former mosque).

The village of **Torrox-Costa**, as elsewhere on the eastern Costa, has more self-catering accommodation than hotels. Once dedicated to fishing and agriculture, it has extensive Roman ruins, but is now an expanding resort with a tourism-based economy.

Nerja

Nerja is the one large international resort to the east of Málaga and it's a popular destination for British, German and Scandinavian visitors. The nightlife is lively, though quieter than in Torremolinos, and the beaches, which are tucked into rocky coves, are prettier, if somewhat smaller. The area also offers good opportunities for hiking, horse-riding, scuba diving, snorkelling and angling, giving Nerja the edge for those seeking an active holiday.

Coastal features at Nerja

The only sight to see in town is the **Balcón de Europa**, a palm-fringed clifftop promenade jutting out over the sea, dividing the sandy crescent of La Caletilla beach on the west from La Calahonda on the east.

Just 6km (4 miles) east of the beach of **Maro** is the famous **Cueva de Nerja** (Cave of Nerja; daily 10am–2pm, 4–6.30pm, 7.30pm in summer; charge; www.cuevadenerja.es). This huge cavern was discovered in 1959 when a group of local boys stumbled on it one day while they were out hunting bats. Floodlights illuminate the impressive limestone formations, which include a stalagmite/stalactite over 32m (105ft) high and 18m (59ft) in diameter. Archaeological remains confirm that these caves were inhabited 30,000 years ago. The Nerja Festival of Music and Dance, held in early July, takes place in the Sala de la Cascada, which has wonderful acoustics.

Inland from Nerja, the corrugated hills of the Sierra de Tejeda rise up toward the village of **Frigiliana**. Under the Moors, it was one of the many prosperous villages within the Kingdom of Granada. Today, the historic centre is regarded as an outstanding example of Moorish village architecture, with a lovely 16th-century church and ruined Moorish castle.

Costa Tropical

After Nerja, the scenery changes dramatically; the mountains begin to cascade to the sea and the panoramas of the ragged coastline are magnificent. Just before La Herradura, a neat little town with a nice beach, road signs proclaim that you are now in the Provincia de Granada. Until you pass into Almería, this part of the Costa del Sol, the most attractive but least known, is officially called the Costa Tropical.

Almuñécar is the first town of any size and has an ancient history. A fine **aqueduct** stands as a monument to the skills of the Roman engineers who constructed it during the reign of Antoninus Pius in the 2nd century AD. A port for Granada in Moorish times, Almuñécar continued to enjoy a certain prestige after the Reconquest when Juan de Herrera, the architect of El Escorial, Philip II's grand monastery-cum-palace near Madrid, was commissioned to design the parish church. These days the town, set around an attractive curving beach, is an increasingly popular family resort. The **Parque Ornitológico Loro Sexi** (Loro Sexi Ornithological Botanic Gardens; summer 11am–2pm, 6–9pm, winter 10am–2pm, 4–6pm, spring and autumn 11am–2pm, 5–8pm; charge), on the slopes

Tropical Fruit

The coast of Granada province provides a perfect microclimate for the cultivation of exotic crops. Until not long ago, there was a thriving sugar refining industry here. You can still buy bottles of locally distilled and there are stands of sugar cane on the coastal plain here but most of the sugar milling machines now adorn roundabouts in Salobreña and Motril (where there is a museum to the vanished industry). Nowadays, the farmers of the 'Costa Tropical' specialise in sub-tropical fruits for the table, especially avocados, mangoes and custard apples (chirimoyas). You'll find all these on sale in shops, markets and at roadside stalls in season.

below the castle, makes for a very colourful visit: there are more than 1,500 birds belonging to 200 species, and ostriches wander around the park.

Along the road from Almuñécar, pretty villas with spectacular coastal views dot the hillsides until, all of a sudden, the scenery changes dramatically. As the coast flattens out, a town of whitewashed houses clinging to the slopes of a rocky, cone-shaped hill comes into view. **Salobreña** is an impressive sight. A Moorish castle, beautifully restored, stands at the top of the town.

Salobreña stands as the gateway to the agriculturally rich *vega* (plain) of the thriving port city of **Motril**. Sugar cane,

Salobreña and its castle

the source of the greenery, used to flourish here. The sugar refineries in the area once earned the town its nickname – Little Cuba. Like Cuba, Motril is known for its rum. Motril and Salobreña have their own extensive beaches and there are many more to come as the road continues eastward.

The next 40km (25 miles) is a conservation area and the least developed of any section of the coast. The small towns and villages, reminiscent of what the rest of the Costa used to be like before the tourist invasion, have only a few hotels, which means that even in midsummer, the beaches are far from overcrowded. What's more, it's possible to be swimming in the Mediterranean while the snow-covered peaks of the Sierra Nevada shimmer in the distance.

This scenery changes, and much for the worse, after **Adra**, an important fishing and fish processing centre. The N340/E15 crosses a vast and dreary plain covered by

Almería's imposing Alcazaba

ugly plastic greenhouses that produce a great deal of Europe's winter vegetables. The road rejoins the coast at **Aguadulce** where tourists, mainly Spanish, enjoy good beaches, new golf courses and marinas. Here, the mountains meet the sea again and the journey on to Almería is short but attractive.

Almería

Rich in history, **Almería** was once the most important city in Moorish Spain. The Almería of today is a pleasant, provincial capital that's worth a visit if your travels take you to the eastern limits of the Costa del Sol.

There are two major sights. One is Abd-er-Rahman III's massive **Alcazaba** (Apr–Oct Tue–Sun 9am–8.30pm, Nov–Mar Tue–Sun 9am–6.30pm; free admission for EU citizens), which looms large on the hilltop above the city. Although an earthquake caused extensive damage in 1522, the crenellated ochre walls and a section of the turreted ramparts stood firm, and now provide wide-ranging vistas over the city and the sea. The second is the forbidding, fortified **Catedral** (Cathedral; Mon–Fri 10am–5pm, Sat 10am–1pm; charge) that stands just inland from the waterfront Paseo de Almería. It was built in the 16th century, when Barbary pirates were terrorising the coast.

Inland from Almería lies one of the most un-European landscapes on the European continent. The **Sierra de Alhamilla** is a desert of barren mountains, rocky ravines and dry gravel riverbeds; spiky agave plants and prickly pears are the only vegetation. The region's uncanny resemblance to the American West made it a popular film location for spaghetti westerns, including such classics as *A Fistful of Dollars* and *The Good, the Bad and the Ugly*. Near the village of Tabernas is an area known as **Mini-Hollywood** (daily 10am–9pm, weekends only in winter), where two of the film sets have been preserved as tourist attractions. Right next door you will find the **Reserva Zoológica** (daily in summer, in winter Sat–Sun 10am–7pm) a safari park featuring many species of Iberian and African creatures including lions, elephants, reptiles and birds.

ACROSS THE MOUNTAINS TO CÁDIZ

For a complete contrast to the sun, sea and sangría atmosphere of the coast, Antequera, Ronda and other 'White Towns' are easily reached from the busiest part of the Costa del Sol. Or you can cross the mountains to Jerez de la Frontera and Cádiz, with their access to the superlative Doñana National Park. The great inland cities of Andalucía are covered in the next section *(see page 62)*.

Antequera and El Torcal

Set in a rich, fertile plain 47km (29 miles) north of Málaga, the market town of **Antequera**, which has been inhabited since prehistoric times, has a cluster of monuments uphill from the tourist information office. Through the 16th-century 'Giants' Arch' gateway (Arco de los Gigantes) is a Renaissance church, the **Real Colegiata de Santa María la Mayor**. Beside it is the entrance to the ruined Muslim castle of the Alcazaba. On the outskirts of town are three enormous **prehistoric burial chambers**: the Dólmen de Menga, probably constructed around 2,500BC, the Dolmen de Viera and the Dólmen del Romeral.

South of Antequera is a well-known beauty spot, the karst limestone formations of **El Torcal**. The rocks here were laid down in the Jurassic period 150 million years ago and since shaped into abstract forms by the movement of the earth and by wind erosion. From the car park and information centre in the middle of El Torcal, follow the 'green' walking route which takes about an hour to complete and takes in the viewpoint of **Las Ventanillas** from which you can even see the North African coast on a clear day.

Limestone formations of El Torcal

Ronda

The opening of an improved road from San Pedro de Alcántara to **Ronda** has ended the isolation of this mountain area and shortened the driving time from the coast to an hour. One of the most spectacularly situated towns in Europe, Ronda sits atop a cliff-bound plateau, cleaved through the middle by a sheer-sided gorge. The older, Moorish part of town (La Ciudad) lies to the south of the ravine, linked by an 18th-century bridge to El Mercadillo, the more modern district that arose after the Christian reconquest.

The gorge, known as **El Tajo**, is a deep and narrow crevasse that plunges 150m (490ft) to the foaming Río Guadalevín, a tributary of the Guadiaro. You can enjoy a superb view of the Tajo and the patchwork of fields beyond from the **Puente Nuevo** (New Bridge), built in 1788, and from the walkways that follow the edge of the gorge.

To see some of Ronda's most important monuments, cross the bridge into **La Ciudad**, the old Moorish enclave which remained impervious to Christian assault until 1485. On one side of the Plaza de Campillo square stands the **Palacio de Mondragón** (open Mon–Fri 10am–6pm, Sat, Sun and hols 10am–3pm; charge), constructed by Abomelic, King of Ronda, in 1314 and later taken over by the Christian conquerors. A distinguished Renaissance portal, a later addition, opens onto spacious courtyards where horseshoe arches and distinctive tile ornaments indicate the Moorish origins of this grand building.

Unspeakable end

During the Spanish Civil War, Nationalist sympathisers in Ronda were hurled to their deaths in the gorge, an event recalled by Ernest Hemingway in his novel *For Whom the Bell Tolls*.

Just a short distance away, Ronda's original mosque survives in the form of the **Iglesia de Santa María la Mayor** (open daily 10am–6pm; charge). The minaret was converted into a bell tower and a Gothic nave was tacked on to the original structure, followed by a high altar in ornate 16th-century Plateresque style and some finely carved baroque choir stalls. The church overlooks the Plaza de la Duquesa de Parcent, the main square, with the long, elegant façade of the **Ayuntamiento** (Town Hall) gracing another side.

Heading back towards the Puente Nuevo, stop to view the exterior of the **Palacio del Marqués de Salvatierra**, an 18th-century mansion famous for its wrought-iron balconies. Nearby stands **La Mina y Jardines de Forestier – Casa del Rey Moro**

Ronda perches precariously above the mighty Tajo Gorge

(The Mine and Forestier Gardens – Moorish King's House; gardens only open to the public daily 10am–7pm; charge), where you will find the remnants of a 14th-century water mine, and gardens designed by the French landscaper Jean Claude Nicolas Forestier in the 1920s. A flight of over 300 steps cut out of the rock in Moorish times leads down from the garden to a spring in the gorge.

Beyond here the road curves down towards the Tajo, where two more bridges – the **Puente Viejo** (Old Bridge), built on Roman foundations, and the Moorish **Puente Arabe** – span the gorge and offer striking views of the chasm. Down by the river stand the **Baños Árabes** (Moor-

Ronda's 18th-century bullring

ish Baths; open Mon–Fri 10am–6pm, Sat, Sun and hols 10am–3pm; charge), its vaulted roof still intact.

Immediately back across the Puente Nuevo, a *parador (see page 106)* occupies what was the old Town Hall and just beyond that is Ronda's famous **Plaza de Toros y Museo Taurino** (Bullring and Bullfighting Museum; Apr–Sept 10am–8pm, Mar and Oct 10am–7pm, Nov– Feb 10am–6pm; charge; www. rmcr.org). Ronda is regarded as the cradle of modern bullfighting, and the bullring is the oldest in Spain, known for its monumental colonade protecting the double-tiered seating.

The White Towns

If one archetypal image of Andalucia is its endless sandy beaches, another is the ubiquitous whitewashed mountain town, a labyrinth of narrow, stepped and winding streets clinging to the hillside or edging up to a crag or cliff. The most attractive white towns and villages are scattered over the mountains between Ronda and the east coast.

One of the most accessible is **Grazalema**, which serves as a service centre for visitors to the nature reserve of the same name. The slopes around Grazalema support forests of the rare Spanish fir, *abies pinsapo*, watered by the highest rate of rainfall in Spain. Across the hills is the handsome white town of **Arcos de la Frontera** – its name hinting at the times when such places stood on the border between

Muslim and Christian dominions. Next to the parish church is a balcony giving dramatic views over the valley below. Other white towns worth linking up in a tour starting out from Ronda are **Setenil de las Bodegas**, **Olvera** and **Zahara de la Sierra**.

Cádiz

The ancient city of **Cádiz**, sitting at the end of a very narrow peninsula of land that runs parallel to the coast, was founded by the Phoenicians in 1100BC and is considered to be Spain's oldest town. In fact, Cádiz's amazing amalgam of history is not readily apparent, with only the remains of the old Roman theatre betraying the city's age. It was reconquered by Alfonso X in 1262 and granted the monopoly of trade with Africa by the Catholic Monarchs in 1493. Columbus also departed from this city on his second and fourth

The beautiful white town of Olvera

The Catedral, Cádiz

voyages in 1493 and 1502 respectively. In the latter part of the 16th century, it twice came under attack by enemy naval forces and a period of prosperity ensued when the Casa de Contratación, the monopoly rights for trade with the Americas, was transferred from Sevilla by order of Felipe V in 1717. A century later, on 19 March 1812, while under attack from Napoleon's forces, the national parliament met in the church of San Felipe Neri and proclaimed the first Spanish parliament.

Of most interest in the town today is the architecturally contrasting baroque and classical **Catedral**, which was constructed between 1772 and 1838. The elegant **Hospital de Mujeres** (Women's Hospital), built even earlier, in 1749, is notable for its patio and art collection, including a fine El Greco. The ceiling of the unusual **Oratorio de la Santa Cueva** church is adorned by five spectacular paintings – three of which are fine examples of Goya's work. The church of **San Felipe Neri**, mentioned above, is also well worth a look.

El Puerto de Santa María

This small town, on the coast of the Bay of Cádiz, looks across to Cádiz and has considerable charm. It is generally overlooked by foreign visitors, but the Spanish flock here in their thousands, especially in August when there are a series of bullfights. At that time, the seafood restaurants, for which El Puerto is famous, are full until the early hours. In fact, there isn't too much to see here, but El Puerto de Santa María is one of those places to be savoured for its atmosphere. Located between Jerez de la Frontera and Cádiz, El Puerto is easily reached by road or rail. However, the nicest way to get here is on the small ferry that plies its way between Cádiz and the dockside in El Puerto.

Jerez de la Frontera

The name **Jerez de la Frontera** is indicative of two things. ◀ It once lay close to the frontier of the old Moorish kingdom of Granada, hence *de la Frontera*. And *Jerez* (pronounced khe-*reth*) gave its name to the wine that has made the town famous, better known to the world as sherry.

Although known as long ago as the Phoenician era, Jerez first came to prominence under the Moors in the 11th–12th century, and it is from that period that the impressively walled and towered **Alcázar** dates. Inside is a simple but elegant mosque that was later converted into a chapel dedicated to Santa María la Real. Reconquered by King Alfonso X in 1264, it became one of the most prosperous towns in Andalucía after the discovery of the Americas and the unification

Bodega tours

Most *bodegas* in Jerez organise guided tours on weekdays. The visits include a full explanation of the cultivation methods and the production process.

Equestrian expertise in the Spanish Riding School

of Spain in 1492. Below the Alcázar is the **Colegiata** (Collegiate Church), a dark stone building dating from the 17th century. Housed within is the image of *Cristo de la Viña* (Christ of the Vineyard).

It was the development of the sherry and brandy business that brought the city worldwide acclaim and more prosperity. It is impossible to miss the *bodegas* of such prestigious old firms as Harvey, Williams & Humbert, Gonzalez-Byass and Pedro Domecq. As some of the names imply, it was a group of English merchants who launched Jerez as the world capital of fortified wine. Three centuries on, their descendants still control the sherry trade.

Jerez is also famous for its horses. The aristocracy built vast ranches alongside its vineyards. The Domecq family established the **Real Escuela Andaluza del Arte Ecuestre** (Spanish Riding School; Mon–Fri 11am–1pm; www.realescuela.org) in 1973 as a showcase for Andalucían equestrian skills. Dressage exhibitions are held on Thursday, but visitors can watch practice sessions on other mornings. The colourful Feria del Caballo (Horse Fair) takes place each May.

Jerez has more subtle attractions, too. In addition to churches and mansions, there's the **Centro Andaluz de Flamenco** in the Palacio Pemartín and the **Museo de Relojes** (Clock Museum; Tue–Sun 10am–3pm, Mar–Oct also Tue–Sat 5–7pm, Nov–Feb mornings only, closed Jan; charge) in its own delightful gardens.

Doñana National Park

Listed as a World Heritage Site, the **Doñana National Park** is probably the most famous park in Spain, with a host of national and international awards to its name. Covering 862 sq km (333 sq miles), it is bordered on one side by the Atlantic Ocean and on another by the Río Guadalquivir, as it winds down from Sevilla to reach the ocean at Sanlúcar de Barrameda.

The Doñana is the last great lowland wilderness sanctuary in southern Europe and has three distinct ecosystems: the *marismas* (salt marshes), the *matorral* (brushwood) and the *dunas* (sand dunes). Within its bounds can be found an amazing array of wildlife, but birds are the main attraction. More than 350 species have been recorded here – and you might have an opportunity to see 170 species in the summer and 220 in winter time. The most popular way to get a general perspective of the Doñana is on a tour organised by Coop. Andaluz Marismas del Rocío, whose large-wheeled buses depart from the visitors' centre at **El Acebuche**. However, for a more detailed understanding, Discovering Doñana (www.discoveringdonana.com), offers half- and full-day tours with professional local guides that are specifically tailored to visitors' interests.

Black-winged stilt at Doñana

The Alcázar Gardens in Sevilla

GREAT CITIES OF ANDALUCÍA

No trip to Andalucía would be complete without seeing at least one of its great inland cities. Sevilla, Córdoba and Granada are repositories of an incredibly rich heritage. The smaller cities of Baeza and Úbeda are also well worth a visit.

Sevilla

The capital of Andalucía, **Sevilla** is the most Spanish of Spanish cities. It is also one of the most beautiful cities in the world, exuding a sensual, spiritual and romantic atmosphere. It was already a thriving riverside settlement when Julius Caesar arrived in 45BC and under the Romans it developed into a major town. Subsequently, Sevilla became the capital of the Visigothic kingdom and then of a Moorish *taifa*, before falling to Fernando III in 1248. A monopoly of trade with the New World brought the city to its peak during the Golden Age.

'Madrid is the capital of Spain,' the saying went, 'but Sevilla is the capital of the world.'

The two most prominent monuments in the city are around the Plaza del Triunfo. Work on the **Catedral and La Giralda** (Mon–Sat 11am–5pm, Sun 2.30–6pm; charge) began in 1401 after the great mosque was razed. The new building followed the ground plan of the old mosque, hence its unusually broad, rectangular form. It is the third-largest Christian church in Europe after St Peter's in Rome and St Paul's in London.

Massive without, and richly decorated within, the cathedral contains over 30 chapels, including the central **Capilla Mayor** with its Flemish altarpiece and the **Capilla Real** (Royal Chapel), the last resting place of Fernando III, the 'King-Saint' who delivered Sevilla from the hands of the infidel. The silver-gilt key to the city, presented to Fernando by the vanquished Moors, can be seen in the treasury, along with a cross made from the first gold brought back from the New World by Columbus. The Great Navigator himself is said to be interred nearby, in the huge, ornate 19th-century sarcophagus by the south entrance.

On the north side of the cathedral lies the **Patio de los Naranjos** (Court of the Orange Trees), the ceremonial courtyard of the old mosque with its original ablutions fountains. The minaret, dating from 1184, was preserved as the bell tower of the cathedral. This celebrated tower, **La Giralda**, is Sevilla's most famous landmark. The exterior is beautifully decorated with typical *sebka* brickwork which contrasts vividly with the bland interior, where a series of 35 gently elevating ramps lead to an observation platform at a height of 70m (230ft) above the ground. This is the finest *mirador* in Sevilla and pro-

Horseplay

To celebrate the recapture of Sevilla by the Christians in 1248, Fernando III of Castile rode his horse to the top of the Giralda.

Two girls on their way to the April Fair

vides stunning views of the old city below. It is surprising to note just how large the Plaza de Toros is when seen from this angle. Look up and you will see how the tower came by its name. In 1356 an earthquake destroyed the original ornamental top and it wasn't until 1558 that the height was raised to 98m (322ft) by the addition of the huge bells and a weathervane (*giralda* in Spanish) in the form of a statue of a beautiful goddess representing Faith.

The **Real Alcázar** (Apr–Sept Tue–Sun 9.30am–7pm, Oct–Mar Tue–Sun 9.30am–5pm; charge; www.patronato-alcazarsevilla.es) is a major monument to mid 14th-century Mudéjar architecture, combining Moorish, Gothic and Renaissance elements. Built by Moorish craftsmen under Christian rule, during the reign of Pedro the Cruel, the rambling palace and its several courtyards incorporate fragments of an earlier Moorish fortress and blend Christian motifs with Moorish designs. You enter on the far side of the square, through the Puerta del León and a visit begins with a tour of the Cuarto del Almirante, where a painting of the Virgen de los Mareantes (Virgin of the Navigators) in the chapel shows Columbus sheltered beneath the Virgin's cloak. The most interesting part is the Patio de las Doncellas (Courtyard of the Maidens), where the rooms preserve outstanding decorative features – ornamental tiles, carved stucco and characteristic coffered ceilings.

The ornate, domed **Salón de Embajadores** (Hall of the Ambassadors) is equal to anything in the Alhambra. Next door is the glass-roofed Patio de las Muñecas (Courtyard of the Dolls), so named for the two tiny human faces carved into the decoration surrounding one of the Moorish arches. These are most unusual, as Muslim craftsmen were forbidden by their religion to depict the human form in their art.

Returning to the entrance courtyard, take the narrow passage on the right to the Patio de María Padilla, which sits on top of underground baths. The apartments beyond are hung with Flemish tapestries recording Carlos V's Tunis Expedition of 1535, one of them showing an upside-down map of the Mediterranean. Not to be missed, either, are the beau-

Seville's April Fair

Seville has two big annual celebrations, both in spring and one after the other. The first is Easter Week, a mixture of religious solemnity and exuberant ostentation. Straight after it comes the hedonistic April Fair (Feria de Abril), which is best thought of as a week-long party extolling all things Andaluz: song and dance, food and drink, horses and bulls. For the duration of the Fair, life in Seville moves across the river from the city centre to a purpose-built fairground – just follow the crowds and you won't get lost. Here, you'll find 'streets' of *casetas*, large pavilions in which private parties are in full swing. A few *casetas*, however, such as those owned by political parties, are open to the public but even if you just stroll around the fairground you'll get much of the flavour of the fiesta. During the day finely dressed men and women parade around in horses and horse-drawn carriages. By evening, after the afternoon's bullfight in the Maestranza bullring, the fairground starts to fill up with people who come to see and be seen, to dance to the sound of flamenco rythms and to drink glasses of chilled fino sherry, the preferred tipple of Andalucía.

The Torre del Oro, constructed in the 13th century

tiful **Gardens**, an oasis of tranquillity in this perpetually busy city.

Nestled around the walls of the Alcázar is the **Barrio de Santa Cruz**, the old Jewish quarter, a picturesque maze of narrow lanes with whitewashed houses and tiny shaded patios that invite leisurely exploration. Just south of the cathedral stands the former exchange building, Casa Lonja, which is now the **Archivo de Indias**. The unusual Cuban wooden shelves are of interest as well as the documents relating to the discovery and conquest of the Americas that rest on them.

Nearby, on the banks of the river, is another of Sevilla's icons. The **Torre del Oro** (Gold Tower; Tue–Fri 10am–2pm, Sat–Sun 11am–2pm; charge) is all that remains of Sevilla's medieval fortifications and in times of possible invasion a huge metal chain was stretched between here and the other river bank to protect the harbour. Originally used to store treasures brought from the Americas, it is now the home to the small **Museo Marítimo** (Maritime Museum). A visit to the **Museo de Bellas Artes** (Museum of Fine Arts; Tue 3–8pm, Wed–Sat 9am–8pm, Sun 9am–2pm; charge) will remind visitors that Sevilla is the birthplace of two of Spain's greatest artists, Velázquez and Murillo.

Another of the city's landmarks is the **Plaza de Toros y Museo Taurino de la Real Maestranza de Caballería** (Bullring and Bullfighting Museum; daily 9.30am–7pm except on days of bullfights when it is open just until 3pm; www. realmaestranza.com). Two of Europe's best-known festivals take place in Sevilla each spring, the **Semana Santa** (Holy Week) parades and the **Feria de Abril** celebration.

Carmona

Carmona, 20km (12 miles) east of Sevilla on the road to Córdoba, sits like a beacon on top of the only hill on an otherwise unrelenting plain. That position has given it strategic importance during its 5,000-year history. It was the Roman era, though, that brought the area prosperity, and the **Museo y Necropolis** (Tue–Fri 9am–6pm, Sat–Sun 9am–3.30pm; free admission for EU citizens) is the largest Roman necropolis outside of Rome.

The town declined after the Romans left, but the Moorish invasion of 713 brought renewed growth and prosperity. The Moors' reign ended in 1247 when Carmona was reconquered by King Fernando II. The town was divided among the victors, principally the orders of Santiago and Calatrava. The 14th and 15th centuries were troubled times as well. The discord was only brought to an end when, in 1630, Felipe IV agreed to grant Carmona the rights of township. The two gates that linked the old Roman road, the **Puerta de Sevilla** and **Puerta de Córdoba**, shouldn't be missed. The former, an unusually shaped small fortress, is very interesting.

Favoured status

Carmona's history is unusual because the town was never under feudal rule, but was protected as a satellite of the crown. That is why it is endowed with such an extraordinary number of palaces, mansions, convents and churches.

Córdoba

These days, Córdoba, a minor provincial city sandwiched between Sevilla and Granada, is often passed over by visitors to Andalucía. But to do so is a considerable mistake. Besides being a very agreeable city, it has fabulous historic connections and an eclectic array of attractions to match. Córdoba was once the largest city in Roman Spain, the capital of the province of Batik and the birthplace of Seneca the Younger, philosopher and tragedian. Its golden era was between the mid-8th and very early 11th centuries, when it was the centre of the great medieval caliphate of Córdoba and one of the world's largest and most cultured cities.

The city is dominated by the greatest surviving monument from that period, the Great Mosque, known as **La Mezquita** (Mon–Sat 8.30am–6pm, Sun 8.30–10am and 2–6pm; charge), which has the distinction of being the oldest monument in day-to-day use in the Western world. Construction was begun in 786, but it was enlarged three times before attaining its present size in 987. It covers an area of 2 hectares (5 acres). Córdoba was reconquered in 1236 and two small Christian chapels were added in 1258 and 1260. In the early 16th century Carlos V decided to construct a cathedral in the centre of the mosque.

Several gateways provide access through the high wall surrounding La Mezquita, the most impressive being the monumental Mudéjar **Puerta del Perdón** (Gate of Forgiveness). Pass through it into the ceremonial forecourt of the **Patio de los Naranjos**, with its fountains and orange trees, to reach the entrance to the mosque. Inside, as your eyes adjust to the dim light, you will see mesmerising rows of columns extending into the shadows in every direction. Antique shafts of crystal-studded porphyry, onyx, marble and jasper, they seem to grow out of the paving stones like trees in an enchanted forest. The double arches overhead, striped in red and white, form a fanciful canopy of curving branches. At the far end, set in the southeast wall, is the splendid 10th-century **mihrab**, lined with marble and gold mosaics, and the **maksourah**, the enclosure where the caliph attended to his prayers. In the central area of the mosque, restorers have exposed a section of the original carved and painted cedar-wood ceiling, which was covered over with vaulting in the 18th century.

The **Catedral**, found at the very centre of the forest of pillars, presents an overpowering contrast to its immediate surroundings. The understated simplicity of Islamic design – and lack of human images – is replaced with an ornate blaze of colour within which human images in either paint, stone, gilt or wood abound. Around the walls more Christian chapels line the perimeter of the mosque.

North of La Mezquita lies the labyrinth of narrow streets that makes up the **Barrio de la Judería** (Jewish Quarter). Some of the best restaurants and *tapas* bars in Córdoba are here. Sights to look for include the Callejón de las Flores (Alley of the

The magnificent pillared interior of La Mezquita

Flowers), lined with houses built around flower-filled patios that are typical of Córdoba, and the 14th-century **Sinagoga** (Tue–Sat 9.30am– 2pm and 3.30–5.30pm, Sun 9.30am–1.30pm) in Calle Judíos. It's a modest affair, just one small room, with a balcony for female worshippers. Córdoba's Jews helped the Moors to gain control of the city in 711 and they lived in peace under the caliphate.

The most illustrious resident of the neighbourhood was the 12th-century philosopher and theologian Moses Maimónides, and his statue stands a few steps from the synagogue in the square named in his honour, **Plaza de Maimónides**. Also here is the **Casa de las Bulas**, which contains El Zoco, a small craft market; and the **Museo Taurino** (Bullfighting Museum; mid-Oct–end Apr Tue–Sat 10am–2pm and 4.30–6.30pm, May–June and Sept–mid-Oct 10am–2pm and 5.30–7.30pm, July–Aug 8.30am–2.30pm; Sun all year 9.30am– 2.30pm; charge).

Northeast of La Mesquita on the Plaza Jerónimo Paéz, the splendid Renaissance Palacio Paéz houses the **Museo Arqueológico de Córdoba** (Tue 2.30–8.30pm, Wed–Sat 9am–8.30pm, Sun 9am–2.30pm). Pride of place goes to objects from the palace of the Moorish city of Medina Azahara *(see opposite)*, such as the bronze stag taken from a fountain presented by Byzantine emperor Constantine VII.

A Christian king, Alfonso XI, built Córdoba's **Alcázar de los Reyes Cristianos**, overlooking the river southwest of the mosque. The ramparts offer a fine view over the old town and the river, the islets in midstream each occupied by a ruined Moorish mill and the ridges of the Sierra de Córdoba low on the northern horizon. The Catholic Monarchs received Columbus and planned the invasion of Granada while resident here.

Other places that are worth a visit are the 16th-century **Palacio de los Marqueses de Viana** and the **Plaza de la**

Corredera. Stroll to the unusual **Plaza del Potro**, which gets its name (Square of the Colt) from the fountain in the centre. The square is home to two interesting museums: the **Museo de Bellas Artes** (Fine Arts Museum; Tue 2.30–8.30pm, Wed–Sat 9am–8.30pm, Sun 9am–2.30pm; charge) and the **Julio Romero de Torres Museum** (16 Sept–15 June Tue–Fri 8.30am–7.30pm, Sat 9.30am–4.30pm, Sun 9.30am–2.30pm; 16 June–15 Sept Tue–Sun 8am–3pm; charge), the latter devoted to the local artist who specialised in mildly erotic paintings of beautiful Córdoban women.

Eight kilometres (5 miles) west of Córdoba lie the ruins of the intriguing **Medina Azahara** (Tue–Sat 10am– 8.30pm, 6.30pm in winter, Sun 10am–2pm; free admission for EU citizens). It was commissioned in 936 by Abd-ar-Rahman III in honour of his favourite concubine, Al Zahra (The Flower). Records indicate that building materials for the grand design

Patio in the Palacio de los Marqueses de Viana

were brought from Constantinople and various North African locations. Despite such auspicious beginnings, it had a short life; the palace was razed with the break-up of the caliphate of Córdoba in the early 11th century. Many of the materials were used on buildings elsewhere. For nearly 900 years, it was left in ruins and only in 1910 did excavation work begin. Today, reconstructions give some impression of the magnificence of this sumptuous complex of baths, schools, gardens and stately apartments, built on three terraces. No public transport runs out here, but the tourist office organises a special bus; ask for the timetable.

Alcalá la Real

The road from Córdoba to Granada is, in many sections, rather dramatic, with mountainous scenery and olive groves (Jaén Province is the world's largest olive-growing area), dot-

The splendid Medina Azahara survived for less than a century

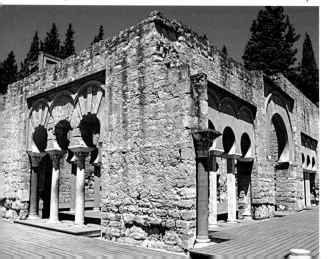

ted with little white-walled towns often crowned with castles. The last sizeable town before Granada, **Alcalá la Real**, was a Moorish fortified city from the early 8th century and remained a strategic bastion until the reconquest of Granada in 1492, after which further Christian monuments were added. The **Fortaleza de la Mota** (daily Jun–Sept 10.30am–1.30pm and 5–8pm, Oct–May 10.30am–1.30pm and 3.30– 6.30pm – tickets sold up to one hour before closing; charge), on the summit at 1,033m (3,389ft), is an amazing complex combining Moorish and Christian influences, and has fabulous views.

Baeza and Úbeda

Two handsome Renaissance towns stand on adjacent hills amid the olive groves northeast of the city of Jaén. **Baeza** is the smaller of the two and has a compact historic centre. Start your tour on foot outside the tourist information office in the Plaza del Pópulo, just off the main square. From here, go uphill towards the cathedral. The building opposite it is a former seminary decorated with elegant, calligraphic graffitti by its students. Heading back downhill you pass the Palacio de Jabalquinto, a magnificent palace with an exquisite Isabelline facade.

Úbeda is an even more impressive repository of great architecture. Its finest buildings are by the architect Andrés de Vandelvira who worked for two wealthy noblemen employed by the king of Spain, Francisco de los Cobos and Juan Vázquez de Molina. The square in the centre of the old part of town is named after the latter of these, the Plaza de Vázquez de Molina. On it stands three remarkable buildings: the church of El Salvador, a mansion converted into a parador hotel and the Palacio de las Cadenas, now the town hall. Worth seeking out in the backstreets is the 14th-century Casa Mudéjar housing Úbeda's archeological museum.

Granada

The Nasrid dynasty rose to power in Granada just as the fortunes of the Spanish Moors were beginning to wane. The first of the line, Mohammed ben Alhamar, established his capital here in 1232, after Fernando III had forced him from Jaén. Two years later, Moors fleeing from vanquished Sevilla swelled the population, which had already been augmented by refugees from Córdoba. Rather than grieve for the homes they had left behind, the industrious Moors set about making Granada the grandest city of Al Andalus. Over the next century, the hilltop palace of the Alhambra took shape. Granada was the last of the great Moorish kingdoms of Andalucía to be reconquered, and King Boabdil's surrender to the Catholic Monarchs in January 1492 marked the end of the Muslim Empire in Spain.

The second most visited monument in Spain is the world-famous **Alhambra and Generalife** (Mar–Oct daily

The mighty Alhambra towers over Granada

8.30am–8pm, Tue–Sat also 10–11.30pm; Nov–Feb daily 8.30am–6pm, Fri–Sat also 8–9.30pm; charge; www.alhambra-patronato.es). Entry is restricted to 6,300 people every day; advance purchase of tickets highly recommended. This can be done 8.30am–2pm at any branch of LA CAIXA bank in Spain, with a small surcharge; by telephone 8am–9pm on 902 888001; or at www.alhambra-tickets.com. Any remaining tickets for each day are sold at the Alhambra ticket office from 8am. The Alhambra takes its name, which means 'the red one', from the red-brown bricks of its outer walls, which rise precipitously above the deep gorge of the Río Darro. Its strategically placed towers command superb views over the city below.

Within the walls of the Alhambra there are four main areas, which are best explored in the following order: the **Alcazaba** (fortress), the **Casa Real Vieja** (Old Royal Palace), the **Casa Real Nueva** (New Royal Palace) and finally the **Generalife** (summer gardens). Amazingly, this complex fell into disrepair over the centuries and was used as a barracks for Napoleon's troops during the Wars of Independence. It wasn't until 1870 that it was designated a National Monument.

The Alcazaba is the oldest part of the Alhambra and only the impressive outer walls and towers survive. The main attraction is the view from the Torre de la Vela, north over the Albaicín and Sacramonte areas of the city and south to the high snow-capped peaks of the Sierra Nevada.

The highlight of the monument is the **Palacio Nazaríes**, the magnificent home of the rulers of the kingdom of Grana-

---

Earthly paradise

In 1494, only two years after the Alhambra had been captured by Christian forces, the German historian, Hieronymus Münzer wrote: 'There is nothing like it in Europe; it is so magnificent, so majestic, so exquisitely fashioned... that one cannot be sure one is not in Paradise.'

da. It is actually a series of palaces, each with its own patios, fountains and other adornments. The intricacy, delicacy and sheer beauty of the design creates a visual impression beyond words.

The **Salón de Embajadores** (Hall of the Ambassadors), or royal audience chamber, is one of the most ornate rooms in the Alhambra. Skirted with geometric tiling, the walls and roof are overlaid with delicately shaped plaster stalactites, reaching 18m (60ft) to the carved and painted wooden ceiling. Verses from the Koran and the name of the 14th-century monarch Yusuf I are woven into the design. Through the tall, arched windows are magnificent views of the Albaicín quarter and the River Darro. The hall exits into the delightful courtyard known as the **Patio de los Arrayanes** (Courtyard of the Myrtles), whose cooling pool is surrounded my myrtle bushes to increase the atmosphere of freshness; note also the arcade of graceful marble columns on the southern side. The **Sala de los Abencerrajes** recalls the aristocratic family of that name, that was accused of disloyalty and collusion with the Christians by Boabdil. The king invited the Abencerrajes to a reception in this room and massacred all 36 of the unsuspecting family members. Also of particular interest are the **Patio de los Leones**, whose name derives

Washington Irving

Irving was an American writer who is best known for *The Sketch Book*, a collection of stories that included such classics as *The Legend of Sleepy Hollow* and *Rip Van Winkle*. From 1826 until 1832, he was attached to the American legation in Spain, where he became fascinated by the legends of Moorish Andalucía. During his stay in Granada, he moved into the apartments of Carlos V while writing *Tales of the Alhambra*, a collection of stories about Granada's Moorish past.

from the splashing fountain in the centre upheld by 12 stone lions, the **Torre de las Damas** (Tower of the Ladies) and the old bath area.

The **Palacio Carlos V**, though imposing, is, as the name implies, relatively new and architecturally at odds with the more ornate older palaces, some of which were destroyed to make way for it. Commissioned by Carlos V in 1527, its square exterior belies a surprisingly elegant two-storey circular patio on the inside. Considered on its own merits, the building must be regarded as a fine example of Renaissance architecture.

The exquisite Patio de Arrayanes

Two museums are housed inside the palace. The first, the **Museo Nacional de Arte Hispano-Musulmán** (Museum of Hispano-Moorish Art; Tue–Sat 9am–2.30pm), displays such evocative artefacts as the throne of the Nasrids, a wooden armchair inlaid with silver and ivory, and the Alhambra Vase, which once graced the Hall of the Two Sisters. The second, the **Museo de Bellas Artes** (Fine Arts Museum; Mar–Oct Tue 2.30–8pm, Wed–Sat 9am–8pm, Sun 9am–2.30pm; Nov–Feb Tue 2.30–6pm, Wed–Sat 9am–6pm, Sun 9am–2.30pm), contains works from the Renaissance to the 20th century.

The **Generalife** is found at the eastern end of the Alhambra fortifications on the neighbouring hillside. A modest summer palace, it is surrounded by beautiful terraced gardens where oleander and roses bloom luxuriantly and delicate fountains and cascades play among the neatly clipped myrtle hedges and avenues of cypresses.

Back down in the city, the most prominent monument is the exquisite **Capilla Real** (Royal Chapel; Mon–Sat 10.15am–1.30pm and 4pm–7.30pm, Sun 11am–1.30pm and 3.30–7.30pm; charge; www.capillarealgranada.com), a Renaissance chapel that serves as the mausoleum of the Catholic Monarchs. The effigies of Fernando and Isabela lie on the right-hand side of the chancel, with those of their daughter Juana La Loca and her husband Felipe El Hermoso on the slightly higher monument on the left. Their mortal remains have been interred in the crypt underneath since 1521, after being ceremonially transferred from the Alhambra. On exhibition in the **sacristy** are mementos of the

Alley in the Albaicín

Catholic Monarchs, including Fernando's sword and Isabela's sceptre and crown, a circle of gold embellished with acanthus scrolls.

The adjacent **Catedral** (Mon–Sat 10.30am–1.30pm and 4–8pm, Sun and hols 4–8pm; charge) next door is large and imposing. A few steps away is the **Alcaicería** area, the old silk bazaar of the Moors. These days, it's a

colourful collection of narrow lanes with a concentration of outlets for handicrafts and souvenirs. Not far away is the **Corral del Carbón** (House of Coal). Dating from the 12th century, it is the oldest Moorish monument in the city and is now a centre for typical Granadino arts and crafts.

The **Albaicín**, the old Moorish district on the hill opposite the Alhambra, has a maze of narrow streets and staircases leading to ancient whitewashed houses and enclosed patios. Down by the Río Darro is the exquisite **Casa de Castril**, home of the Archaeological Museum, and the nearby 11th-century **El Bañuelo** (Moorish Baths). Further up the hill is the **Mirador San Nicolás**. From here, you get the best view of the Alhambra, with the majestic Sierra Nevada in the background – a scene replicated on countless postcards.

Guadix

About 50km (32 miles) east of Granada on the road to Murcia is **Guadix**, a particularly unusual city in that many of its inhabitants are troglodytes. In the Barrio de las Cuevas are streets of houses with small front yards that are indistinguishable from ordinary homes. Look closely, though, and

Air-dried hams in Trevélez

the white, circular chimneys emanating from the rocks give the game away. These are actually caves with a practical use: they're cool in summer and warm in winter. There is plenty more of interest here, including a Moorish castle dating from the 10th and 11th centuries and many important palaces, houses and churches.

LAS ALPUJARRAS

The **Sierra Nevada National Park** has the distinction of having the highest peak on the Spanish mainland (Mulhacén is 3,482m/11,420ft high), as well as a wide diversity of flora made possible by the nearby Mediterranean Biosphere Reserve. It also has the highest road in Europe; along it is the Solynieve (literally Sun and Snow) ski resort, accessible all year round at some 2,500m (8,000ft), and Pico Veleta (Weathercock Peak) at 3,398m (11,148ft), which can only be reached in the summer.

Over the mountains from Granada, on the southern flanks of the range, is **Las Alpujarras**, a pretty area of steep hillsides and deep valleys dotted with towns and villages that retain more than a flavour of the traditional Moorish settlement. Their architecture of eccentrically shaped houses with flat gravel spread roofs sprouting eccentric chimneys takes you immediately back to a time when buildings were adapted to the contours not the other way round. Often houses cross over the streets and join each other, creating shady passageways and tunnels. The way of life here in the early 20th century was described by Gerald Brenan in his book, *South from Granada*. More recently the Alpujarras were the backdrop for Chris Stewart's bestseller *Driving Over Lemons*.

The main access to Las Alpujarras is from the Granada to Motril road, the same route along which the defeated Moors travelled on their way into exile. Even today, there is a pass 12km (8 miles) south of Granada that bears the sad name **El Suspiro del Moro** (The Sigh of the Moor). It is from here that distant Granada finally fades from view and it is said that the defeated King Boabdil sighed with regret as he looked back at the city. His mother apparently had little sympathy and is reported to have told him: 'Don't cry like a woman for something you could not defend as a man.'

Church belltower in the Alpujarras

Places to head for include **Trevélez**, the highest village in Spain, famous for its delicious *jamón serrano* (dried cured ham). **Lanjarón** is familiar throughout Spain as the name on the red, green and white label on bottles of water originating from the town's springs. Incidentally, that same water runs free from the *fuentes* (fountains) of many Alpujarras villages; some of the prettiest of them are **Pampaneira**, **Bubión** and **Capileira**.

WHAT TO DO

SPORTS

Most visitors to the Costa del Sol do not plan daytime activities that are any more energetic than lazing on the beach, and save their energy for nightlife. However, sports facilities are there in abundance for those who want to work off the effects of too much paella.

Water Sports

The main resort beaches offer all kinds of sports equipment for hire, as well as beach umbrellas and loungers, and the larger beach restaurants have toilet facilities; some provide changing rooms.

Swimming: With more than 160km (100 miles) of beaches, the Costa del Sol offers plenty of spots for swimming. Most of the sandy strands lie to the west of Málaga, while shingle and rocks (with some sandy coves) predominate to the east. In the high season, the most popular beaches are mobbed. You stand the best chance of finding a patch of sand to yourself to the east of Nerja and west of Estepona. Many beaches now fly the blue flag, which means that water quality and general sanitation meet the EU's environmental standards.

Boating: There are numerous marinas along the coast between Málaga and Sotogrande, providing year-round moorings for yachts and motor boats. Some offer boats for day rentals and longer-term charters (with or without skipper and crew). Marbella has three such establishments and many of the beaches and larger beach hotels rent out sailing boats.

Waterskiing: The main resorts all have waterskiing schools,

Tarifa is world-renowned for its windsurfing

and most big hotels offer instruction. Prices are generally high, but they vary. Swimming and skiing areas often overlap.

Windsurfing: This sport is the coast's fastest-growing activity, with boards, sails and professional instruction available in most of the resort areas. The season runs from March to November with strongest winds in June and September.

Snorkelling and Scuba Diving: Snorkelling can be an engrossing activity, particularly off the rocky, indented stretch of coast beyond Nerja. If you dive or snorkel any distance from shore, you are legally required to tow a marker buoy. Diving centres operate in several resorts. For more information, contact the local tourist office *(see page 128)*.

Angling: Fishing from the rocks and breakwaters is a popular pastime with local people and no permit is required. The deeper waters offshore teem with tunny (tuna), swordfish and shark. Deep-sea fishing boats can be hired at the marinas and many resort hotels can make arrangements for fishing expeditions. A very popular inland fishing spot is the Pantanos del Chorro (*pantano* means reservoir) at the Chorro Dam north of Málaga. Freshwater anglers must have a permit – ask at the nearest tourist office for information on how to obtain one.

Fishing from a breakwater

Other Sports

Golf: When it comes to variety, few resort areas in the world can compare with the Costa del Sol. There are some 30 18-hole courses between Málaga and Gibraltar. Most private and hotel clubs welcome non-residents or non-members, though some may charge visitors a higher fee. Clubs, caddies and carts are generally available for hire. The quality of the courses is excellent – many have been designed by famous names such as Robert Trent Jones and Seve Ballesteros. Las Brisas, near Marbella, has staged the Spanish Open and Valderrama, near Sotogrande, has hosted the Ryder Cup. Though a private club, Valderrama (www.valderrama.com) is open to the public after 10.30am (green fees are €300 on weekdays and €320 at weekends). For details of golf courses and fees, consult the website of the Spanish Golf Federation, www.golfspain federacion.com.

Cycling through the Sierra de Cazorla

Tennis: The climate of southern Spain is ideal for tennis and many hotels have their own courts for the use of guests. If yours doesn't, there is likely to be a municipal sports centre nearby with courts available for hire. The main resorts also have private tennis clubs where you can ask about temporary membership.

Cycling: Bikes can be hired at towns up and down the coast and inland (where mountain roads and trails are ideal for mountain-biking).

Hiking: There are a number of good hiking areas within easy reach of the coast, notably the Parque Nacional Montes de Málaga just north of Málaga and the impressive limestone formations of El Torcal de Antequera a little further inland *(see page 53)*. For more good walks, try the area around Ronda, and the hills above the Refugio de Juanar near Marbella *(see page 40)*.

Horse Riding: Andalucía is famous for both horses and horsemanship. There are stables on the coast and near the inland cities, with mounts for hire; you can canter along the open beach or ride up into the hills.

Skiing: Skiing can be enjoyed between December and May at the Solynieve resort in the Sierra Nevada near Granada, 160km (100 miles) northeast of Málaga. Situated near the summit of Mt Veleta, it is Europe's southernmost ski resort.

SHOPPING

Most shops are open from 9.30 or 10am–1.30 or 2pm and from 5–8pm. The siesta *(see below)* is still religiously observed in southern Spain. But in summer, shops in the tourist resorts stay open throughout the day until 8.30pm or later. Department stores and supermarkets do not close for the siesta.

Siesta

The siesta is an afternoon nap taken to avoid the hottest part of the day. It means that many shops and businesses take a three-hour lunch break, closing from 1 or 2pm till 4 or 5pm, and then opening up again until 8pm. This age-old custom seems to be dying out in some parts of northern Spain, but it is still observed in the towns and villages of Andalucía.

Where to Shop

The larger cities offer lower prices and a better selection of goods than resorts like Torremolinos or Fuengirola. The El Corte Inglés department store, with branches in Málaga, Sevilla and other places, is also well worth looking for.

For more sophisticated shopping, nothing can compare with Marbella or Puer-

The characterful Barrio de Santa Cruz in Sevilla

to Banús, where dozens of attractive harbourfront boutiques offer a stunning selection of merchandise at equally stunning prices. You can make a considerable saving on luxury goods like jewellery, watches, perfumes and Havana cigars in duty-free Gibraltar, where there is no VAT (called IVA in Spain).Ceuta, the Spanish protectorate on the North African coast, has special tax status. Alcohol, for example, is vastly cheaper there than in mainland Spain.

Markets
Weekly open-air markets are held on Monday in Marbella, Tuesday in Nerja and Fuengirola, Wednesday in Estepona, Thursday in Torremolinos and San Pedro de Alcántara, and Friday in Benalmádena. Most cities have a *rastro* (flea market) on Sunday morning. Of these, Sevilla's is the largest and the town also has a coin-and-stamp and small animal market on the same day.

Fans for sale

What to Buy

Traditional Spanish handicrafts are high on any souvenir-hunter's shopping list.

Ceramics: Everyday glazed terracotta pottery can be bought all along the coast. There is also a wide selection of tiles *(azulejos)*, vases, bowls and jugs, with floral or geometric decorations in bright colours.

Foodstuffs: Take home a taste of Spain with some olives, olive oil, almonds, cheese or mouthwatering biscuits.

Jewellery: Silver rings, bracelets and necklaces in modern designs make good buys, as do the artificial Majorica pearls of Spain. Look, too, for fine filigree jewellery from Córdoba, and smooth, polished olive-wood beads.

Leather and Suede: Choose from a wide selection of handbags, belts, wallets, trousers, skirts, shoes and coats. Leather goods still compare favourably in price with Italian- and French-made articles, and the local factories turn out stylish, high-quality leather clothing. Córdoba, which has been producing leather goods since Roman times, is famous for its embossed leather. But beware: many of the leather goods you will see for sale have been imported from Morocco and are sold at inflated prices. It's actually cheaper, and much more interesting, to take a day trip to Tangier and buy such goods there.

Souvenirs: Often delightfully tacky, from plastic castanets and flamenco dolls to imitation wineskins *(botas de vino)* and even bullfight posters printed with your own name.

Wine and Spirits: Sweet Málaga wine, sherry, brandy and Spanish wines provide some of the best bargains in Spain, and are generally cheaper when bought in a supermarket than at the airport.

ENTERTAINMENT

Tour operators offer any number of excursions, some more esoteric than others, with brochures and booking facilities available through your hotel or a local travel agent.

Bullfights: Andalucía is famed for its bullfighting traditions, and has two of the seven first-class *Plazas de Toros* (bullrings) in Spain (in Sevilla and Córdoba). The provincial capitals of Almería, Granada, Huelva, Jaén and Málaga as well as Algeciras and El Puerto de Santa María have second-class rings. All others fall into the third class. The two main events are a *corrida de toros*, where fully qualified matadors fight fully grown *toros* (bulls), of at least four years

Matador statue in Ronda

old; and *novilladas*, where *novilleros* (novice matadors) fight *novillos* (immature bulls).

As a rule of thumb, the better events are held in the better plazas, particularly during the *ferias* (fairs) in the major cities. Equally true is the fact that most of the events held in the resort towns are mainly for the benefit of tourists and are of lesser quality – although they are not generally less expensive. Outside of the *ferias* – when they are held daily – only Sevilla has bullfights on a regular basis. In other places, with the exception of Easter Sunday and 15 August – important national holidays – they are held sporadically and advertised by way of the ubiquitous *carteles* (posters) stuck on every wall. The perceived cruelty of bullfights arouses very strong feelings among Americans and northern Europeans. They are, however, very much part of the southern Spanish culture.

Flamenco: All the coastal resorts offer flamenco shows for tourists. They can be highly entertaining, but they are more in the spirit of show business than true flamenco. To experience flamenco at its most authentic, you will have to search out bars and small clubs in Málaga, Granada or Sevilla. Ask the local tourist office for advice on where to go.

The Sound of Andalucía

Flamenco is an ancient art form, combining elements of Visigothic, Moorish and Gypsy music. There are two distinct types; the *cante jondo* (deep song), an intense outpouring of emotion; and the animated *cante chico* (light song). There are also different varieties of flamenco dance, including the *tango, fandango, farruca* and *zambra*, performed to the staccato rhythms and counter-rhythms of the castanets, hand clapping (*palmadas*) and finger snapping (*pitos*), as well as furious heel-drumming (*zapateado*). There is no need to understand Spanish to enjoy the spectacle – you simply have to feel the music.

Discos and Nightclubs: Some discos open as early as 9pm, but most don't gear up for business until 11pm or midnight. They close late, too, around 4am or even later. Nightclubs *(salas de fiesta)* usually stage two shows an evening, one at about midnight or 1am and the other around 3am. Depending on the club, the show may feature flamenco performances, drag acts, or shows with semi-nude women. Bars, pubs and clubs often provide musical entertainment.

Flamenco in Córdoba

Casinos: There are two gambling establishments that operate from 8pm to the early hours: Casino Torrequebrada (www.casinotorrequebrada.net) in Benalmádena-Costa, and Casino Marbella (www.casinomarbella.com), under the Hotel Andalucía Plaza in Puerto Banús. In addition to the usual games, the casinos have a bar, restaurant and nightclub on the premises. Formal dress (jacket and tie for men) is required. Don't forget to bring your passport for identification.

Concerts: From May to October, Tívoli World (www.tivoli.es) brings the stars of rock and pop to Torremolinos for concerts in the open air. The season's programme may include performances of flamenco and *zarzuela* (Spanish light opera). In winter, Málaga's symphony orchestra performs in the Teatro Cervantes theatre (www.teatrocervantes.com), and guest artists appear at Castillo El Bil-Bil in Benalmádena-Costa.

ACTIVITIES FOR CHILDREN

The Costa del Sol is an ideal place for families with kids – it is, after all, one long beach. Apart from paddling and sand-castles, older children can learn how to sail, waterski or windsurf. Alternatively, there are the **water parks** at Mijas, Torremolinos and Estepona. Further diversions include the **aquariums** in Benalmádena and Puerto Banús, the display of birds of prey at the top of the cable car in Benalmádena, the Cueva (cave) de Nerja, and **Mini-Hollywood** near Almería. In the evening, **Tívoli World** (www.tivolicostadelsol.com) near Benalmádena provides all the fun of the fair, with rides

Hooded penitents in Sevilla

and a roller coaster, and there's a bar and flamenco show for adults. **Crocodile Park** (www.crocodile-park. com), situated just north of Málaga, will intrigue most children, as will the horse shows at **El Ranchito** (www. ranchito.com) in Benalmád-ena and at the Escuela de Arte Ecuestre Costa del Sol in Estepona (www.escuela-ecuestre.com.

Children are especially vul-nerable to the sun so take high-factor sunscreen and sun hats and make sure they are covered up during the middle of the day, and wear T-shirts in the water (a siesta during the hottest part of the day is a good idea).

Calendar of Events

January: *Cabalgata de Reyes* (Three Kings' Parade), Málaga. On 5 January, the eve of Epiphany, floats, bands and traditionally costumed characters commemorate the visit of the Wise Men to the infant Christ.

March/April: *Semana Santa* (Holy Week), throughout the area. Sombre processions of hooded penitents and religious images every night during the week before Easter. Most impressive in Sevilla, Málaga and Granada.

April: *Feria de Abril* (April Fair, starts 10 days after Easter), Sevilla. Horses and riders, bullfights, flamenco, fireworks and street parties are part of Andalucía's most colourful festival.

April/May: *Feria del Caballo* (Horse Fair), Jerez de la Frontera. Spain's equestrian showcase, including racing, dressage and carriage competitions.

May: *Romería de San Isidro* (Pilgrimage of St Isidore), Estepona. Decorated carts and costumed riders parade. *Dia de la Cruz*, Granada. Decorated crosses and folk dancing. *El Rocio* (Whitsun, May/June). Famous pilgrimage to a shrine on the dge of Doñana National Park.

June: *Corpus Cristi*, throughout the area. Bullfights and fireworks enliven this national holiday, a big event in Granada.

June/July: *Festival Internacional de Música y Danza*, Granada. Concerts and dance performed outdoors in the Alhambra and Generalife.

July: *Virgen del Carmen*, coastal towns. Processions of fishing boats pay tribute to the Virgin of Carmen, protector of fishermen.

August: *Feria de Málaga* (Málaga Fair), Málaga. A carnival, circus, bullfights and flamenco events enliven the first fortnight of the month. *Festival de España*, Nerja. The town's famous cave provides the eerie venue for this subterranean celebration of music and dance.

September: *Feria de Ronda* (Ronda Fair), Ronda. The highlight of this fair is the *corrida goyesca*, a costumed bullfight. *Fiesta de la Vendímia* (Wine Harvest Festival), Jerez de la Frontera. A parade, bullfights, flamenco and equestrian events follow the blessing of the grape harvest.

December 28: *Fiesta de Verdiales*, Málaga. Groups from all over the province gather to celebrate this early style of folk song and dance.

EATING OUT

You could easily spend your entire holiday on the Costa del Sol without ever sitting down to a real Spanish meal. In the big coastal resorts the range of eating places is amazing: hamburger stands, pizza bars, pub grub, beach barbecues and restaurants of almost any nationality you can think of, with a few Spanish ones thrown in for good measure. In fact, you could eat bacon and eggs, beans on toast, steak and chips and other standard British fare every day, without going into the same restaurant twice. But for those visitors keen to sample the delights of the local cuisine, there are numerous fine Spanish restaurants on the coast and many more throughout Andalucía.

WHERE TO EAT

One of Spain's most civilised institutions is the **tapas** bar, or *tasca*. Originally, the idea was that when you ordered a drink, generally beer or wine only, a small helping of a tasty morsel and a couple of pieces of bread were given free. The food was served on a small plate, traditionally used to cover the glass, and came to be called a *tapa*, which literally means lid. These days such authentic bars, with free morsels, are hard to find. There is very often a charge, which varies depending on what you choose. Although this is still a fine way of sam-

Late eating

First-time visitors to Spain are often surprised by the late eating hours: the Spanish rarely sit down to lunch (*almuerzo*), which is the main meal of the day for locals, before 2pm and dinner (*cena*) starts around 9.30 or 10pm. However, in the resort areas many restaurants stay open throughout the day.

El Peñon restaurant overlooks the beach in Salobreña

pling a number of different dishes, it can easily become cost-lier than selecting an inexpensive *menú del día* (set menu).

Cafeterías are middle-range establishments, common in the resorts, usually offering a selection of *platos combinados* (combination dishes), such as a pork chop and chips, or squid and salad, with bread and a drink included.

A **comedor**, literally 'dining room', is often a small area at the back of a bar where you can sit down and dig into a basic but satisfying meal. *Comedores* tend to cater to local work-ers: cheap and cheerful, they are usually open for lunch only.

Restaurantes proper are pretty much the same as anywhere else; they are usually open for lunch and dinner, and close during the afternoon and one day a week. They may offer a *menú del día* which will be much cheaper than ordering à la carte. A restaurant calling itself a *marisquería* specialises in shellfish and seafood, while an *asador* is the place for roast meats. A *venta* is a small, family-run restaurant serving down-to-earth country fare, and is well worth looking out for if you venture away from the coast. *Chiringuitos*, either permanent or just erected for the summer, are beachside restaurants that vary in size and quality; some of the most interesting are found on the coastline of the Costa Tropical.

WHAT TO EAT

Breakfast

Spaniards normally eat a light breakfast of cereal and toast or a *tostada con aceite* (toasted roll with olive oil) washed down with *café con leche* (milky coffee). Spanish espresso *(café solo)* is strong stuff, even with a touch of milk *(un cortado)*. Resort hotels often offer a full buffet breakfast and, of course, a full English breakfast isn't hard to find.

A light lunch with wine

Tapas and Snacks

Every good bar offers a selection of tapas. Among the dozens of items to choose from, you may find sweet red peppers in olive oil seasoned with garlic, Russian salad, slices of sausage (both spicy *chorizo* and paprika-flavoured *salchichón*), *jamón serrano* (cured ham), marinated mussels, baby squid, clams or *tortilla de patatas* (Spanish omelette, with potato and onion filling, usually served cold in slices). For a larger portion of any given tapa, ask for a *ración*. If you feel that's too much for you, order a *media ración*. Late-night revellers often stop at a *kiosko* for a snack of *churros y chocolate* (doughnut-like fritters and thick, sweet, drinking chocolate) on their way home.

Soup of the day

Be sure to try the mixed fish or shellfish soups, *sopa de pescado* and *sopa de mariscos*. Like its French counterpart, the Mediterranean *bouillabaisse*, *sopa marinera* is based on the day's catch and seasoned with tomato, onion, garlic and a dash of white wine or brandy.

Soups

Andalucía's most famous speciality is the cold soup known as *gazpacho*. There are literally dozens of ways to make it, but the version you are likely to find in southern Spain is a chilled blend of cucumber, tomato, and crushed garlic, occasionally accompanied by freshly diced green pepper, tomato, cucumber, chopped hard-boiled egg and fried croutons on the side.

Originally from Málaga, *ajo blanco* (white garlic soup) is a variation on the more common *gazpacho* theme. Ground almonds and garlic form the base of this summer refresher, served ice-cold with a garnish of almonds and grapes.

Vegetable Dishes

The Spanish usually eat vegetables as a first course, rather than as an accompanying dish. Two good specialities of Andalucía are: *alcachofas a la Montilla* – artichoke leaves cooked in a mixture of wine and beef broth, thickened with flour and seasoned with mint, garlic and saffron; and *Judías verdes con salsa de tomate* – green beans in tomato sauce laced with garlic.

Egg Dishes

Egg dishes make popular starters, and a whole Spanish omelette is a filling lunch on its own. *Tortillas* (omelettes) may be filled with asparagus, tuna or mushrooms. *Huevos a la flamenca* is a baked dish of eggs cooked on a base of tomato, garlic and herbs – usually accompanied by diced ham or spicy *chorizo* sausage, fresh peas and sweet red peppers.

Seafood

The seafood you are served in the waterfront restaurants was probably landed on the beach that very morning by the fishermen whose boats lie hauled up on the sand.

The traditional lunch on the coast is sardines skewered on a wooden spike and grilled over a charcoal fire on the beach. This simple but tasty dish is irresistible and extremely good value. Squid may be an interesting option, either cooked in its own ink *(calamares en su tinta)*, a spicy dish, or simply dipped in batter and fried, and served with a twist of lemon. *Gambas* and *cigalas* are large juicy prawns – choose your

Paella

Spain's most famous dish, which the Spaniards usually eat at lunchtime, deserves to be discussed separately. The main ingredient of paella is saffron-flavoured rice, cooked with olive oil, seafood and chicken. But every cook has his or her own variation on this colourful dish that originated in Valencia on Spain's eastern coast. The name paella derives from the flat, round metal pan in which it is cooked.

The secret of perfect paella is fresh ingredients; fresh seafood such as *langosta* (spiny lobster), *langostinos* (a kind of prawn), *cigalas* (giant prawns or sea crayfish), *gambas* (prawns), mussels, clams together with chicken or rabbit, peas, sweet peppers and artichoke hearts, all cooked together slowly as the rice absorbs the juices.

own from the display and have them grilled while you select your wine.

Langosta (lobster) is excellent served hot with butter or cold with mayonnaise. *Boquerones* (fresh anchovies) and *chanquetes* (whitebait) are tossed in flour and deep-fried whole. *Boquerones* may also be prepared ceviche-style, marinaded raw in oil and lemon with garlic and parsley. *Merluza*, or hake, may be served fried, boiled or mushroom-stuffed, perhaps with tomatoes and potatoes. *Besugo* (sea bream) is a high-quality fish, which is brushed with olive oil and simply grilled.

Chargrilled sardines

Other common items on the menu may include *pez espada* (swordfish), *mero* (sea bass), *bonito* (tuna) and *rape* (monkfish). If you have difficulty deciding what to try, you may want to plump for the *fritura malagueña*, a mixed fish fry that includes all of the above. Note that any of these delicacies are priced on the menu for a 100-g (approximately 4-oz) portion, so what appears to be an inexpensive dish may prove very costly.

Chicken and Meat

Spanish chicken is delicious, whether fried, roasted or braised in white wine or sherry with almonds. The staple *arroz con pollo* (chicken with rice) is tasty. Many traditional meat dishes make use of offal such as tripe, brains and sweetbreads.

Riñones al Jerez, kidneys sautéed with sherry, or *rabo de toro*, braised oxtail served in a rich tomato sauce with carrots and spices, are typical of the cuisine of Andalucía. *Ternera a la Sevillana*, veal in a sherry sauce with green olives, is a speciality of Sevilla. Rabbit *(conejo)* or hare *(liebre)* in white wine forms the basis of many a tasty casserole. Steak and various cuts of beef are also available. A local variation on this international standard is *bistec a la mantequilla de anchoas* (beefsteak with an anchovy butter sauce).

Cheese and Dessert

Spaniards eat cheese *(queso)* – notably the tangy *queso manchego* and the milder *queso de Burgos* – after the main course. You may also come across *queso de cabrales*, a combination cheese from the northwestern province of Asturias made from goat's, cow's and sheep's milk. After ageing, it becomes blue-veined and has a sharp taste similar to Roquefort. *Idiázabal* is a smoked and cured goat's cheese.

Fruits in season include *uvas* (grapes), *higos* (figs), *melón* (melon), *naranjas* (oranges), *melocotones* (peaches), *chirimoyas* (custard apples), *fresas* (strawberries) and *cerezas* (cherries). Besides ice cream, southern Spain offers pastries and cream desserts in abundance. One appealing preparation is *brazo de gitano* (gypsy's arm), a rolled sponge cake with rum-flavoured cream filling. The ubiquitous *flan*, or egg and caramel custard, appears on menus all over Spain. Eggs cooked with sugar make a thickened custard called *natillas*.

Grapes on the vine

Wine and Spirits

The white wines of Rioja are very drinkable, but the Rioja reds are the glory of Spain; the aged Gran Reservas (at least five years old) are comparable to some of France's noblest red wines, though Riojas have a character all of their own. Labels to look out for include Marqués de Riscal, Siglo, Cune, Berberana and Campo Viejo.

Navarra, north of the Ebro Valley, produces some interesting red wines (look for Campanas, Señorío de Sarría and Murchante). From La Mancha, between Madrid and Andalucía, come light, crisp Valdepeñas wines.

Pouring sherry in Jerez

Reds and whites from Catalonia will also appear on wine lists. Labels to look for include Torres and Rene Barbier. Many restaurants have their own inexpensive table wine *(vino de la casa)* that can prove to be a less expensive, but still acceptable alternative. Catalonia also produces a sparkling wine, called *cava*. Some varieties may be rather sweet for northern palates but the Cordorniu or Freixenet *brut* (very dry) *cava* are both excellent.

Sangría, the iced combination of red wine and brandy with lemon, orange and apple slices, makes a great refresher, although its sweet and innocent taste can mask its strength.

An aristocrat among wines, *Jerez* (sherry) is produced from grapes grown in the chalky vineyards around Jerez de la

Frontera. It is aged in casks by blending the young wine with a transfusion of mature sherry, a method known as *solera*. *Fino*, the driest of sherries, is a light, golden aperitif that should be served chilled. A type of *fino* called *manzanilla* is slightly richer; Sanlúcar de Barrameda *manzanilla* is especially good. *Amontillado*, usually medium dry, is a deeper gold in colour, and is heavier than a true *fino*. *Amoroso* is medium sweet, with an amber colour, and *oloroso* is still more full-bodied. Cream sherries are not popular in Spain.

Andalucía produces several other semi-sweet to sweet wines, most notably the mahogany-coloured wine of Málaga, called *Málaga Dulce* (rather like port). Sherry-type wines are also made in the Montilla-Moriles region near Córdoba.

Spanish brandy, or *coñac*, tends to be heavy, but it is usually drinkable and reasonably priced. The more expensive brands are much smoother.

A dish full of paella

To Help You Order

Could we have a table?	**¿nos puede dar una mesa?**
Do you have a set menu?	**¿tiene un menú del día?**
I'd like a/an/some …	**quisiera …**

beer	**una cerveza**	milk	**leche**
bread	**pan**	mineral water	**agua mineral**
coffee	**un café**	napkin	**una servilleta**
cutlery	**los cubiertos**	potatoes	**patatas**
dessert	**un postre**	rice	**arroz**
fish	**pescado**	salad	**una ensalada**
fruit	**fruta**	sandwich	**un bocadillo**
glass	**un vaso**	sugar	**azúcar**
ice cream	**un helado**	tea	**un té**
meat	**carne**	(iced) water	**agua (fresca)**
menu	**la carta**	wine	**vino**

… and Read the Menu

aceitunas	olives	**judías**	beans
albóndigas	meatballs	**lenguado**	sole
almejas	baby clams	**mariscos**	shellfish
atún	tuna	**mejillones**	mussels
bacalao	cod	**ostras**	oysters
besugo	sea bream	**pastel**	cake
bistec	steak	**pimiento**	sweet red
calamares	squid		pepper
callos	tripe	**pollo**	chicken
cangrejo	crab	**pulpitos**	baby octopus
cerdo	pork	**salchichón**	salami
champiñones	mushrooms	**salmonete**	red mullet
chuletas	chops	**salsa**	sauce
cordero	lamb	**ternera**	veal
entremeses	hors-d'œuvres	**tortilla**	omelette
gambas	prawns	**trucha**	trout
huevos	eggs	**uvas**	grapes

HANDY TRAVEL TIPS

An A–Z Summary of Practical Information

A

ACCOMMODATION *(hotel; alojamiento;*
see also CAMPING, YOUTH HOSTELS and RECOMMENDED HOTELS)

If you are travelling independently, you will find a wide range of accommodation in the Costa del Sol. For a comprehensive listing of accommodation and rates throughout Spain, consult the *Guía Oficial de Hoteles*, available from bookshops and newsagents. By law, room rates must be posted in every hotel's reception area and rooms. Meals (including breakfast) are not usually included in this rate, and VAT (IVA in Spanish) will be added to your bill.

Establishments are graded by each of Spain's 17 autonomous governments according to the following system, with one of the following classifications plus a starred rating, depending on the amount, kind and quality of services offered:

Hotel (H): Rated between one and five stars. The most expensive option, topped only by Hotel 5-star Gran Lujo (GL), signifying top-of-the-range accommodation.

Hotel Residencia (HR): Same as a hotel, but without a restaurant.

Motel (M): Very similar to a hotel, but in reality these establishments are few and far between.

Hotel Apartamentos (HA): Apartments within hotels and rated the same as a hotel.

Residencia Apartamentos (RA): Residential apartments without a restaurant, rated the same as a hotel.

Hostal (HS): A more modest hotel, often family-owned and operated, and rated between one and three stars. Rates overlap with the lower range of hotels, eg, a three-star *hostal* usually costs about the same as a one- or two-star hotel.

Hostal Residencia (HSR): Similar to a *hostal*, but with no restaurant.

Pensión (P): A boarding house, rated between one and three stars, with only basic amenities.

Ciudad de Vacaciones (CV): A hotel complex with sports facilities.

Casa Rural: Country house offering bed-and-breakfast or self-catering accommodation.

Parador: A state-run hotel, often in a castle or other historic building. Advance booking is not essential but is highly recommended for the most popular paradors. For information and bookings in the UK, contact Keytel International, 402 Edgware Road, London W2 1ED, tel: 020 7616 0300, www.keytel.co.uk. In the USA and Canada, contact Marketing Ahead, 381 Park Avenue South, Suite 718, New York, NY 10016, tel: 800-223-1356 or 212-686-9213, fax: 212-686-0271, www.marketingahead. com. In Spain, contact the Paradores de Turismo, Central de Reservas, Requena 3, 28013 Madrid, tel: 902 547 979, fax: 902 525 432, www.parador.es.

I'd like a single/double room	**Quisiera una habitación individual/doble**
with bath/shower	**con baño/ducha**
What's the rate per night?	**¿Cuál es el precio por noche?**

AIRPORTS (aeropuerto; see also GETTING THERE)

The Costa del Sol is served by Málaga's **Aeropuerto Internacional** (tel: 902 404 704, www.aena.es), situated some 8km (5 miles) west of the centre of Málaga and 7km (4½ miles) from Torremolinos. There is a bus service every 20 minutes to Málaga, Torremolinos and Benalmádena Costa (tel: 902 143 144, www.csta-portillo. com for timetables), as well as a train service (tel: 902 240 202, www.renfe.es; follow the signs marked *ferrocarril*) to central Málaga and the coastal resorts from Torremolinos to Fuengirola. Taxis can be found at the taxi rank outside the terminal. The journey from the airport to central Málaga or Torremolinos takes about 10 to 15 minutes, and about 20 minutes to Fuengirola.

Other airports with international flights serving the region are at Granada, Almería, Sevilla's San Pablo (for all Spanish airports tel: 902 404 704, www.aena.es), and Gibraltar (tel: 350 730 26). Buses operate between the latter and the Puerta de Jerez, directly in front of the impressive Hotel Alfonso XIII.

B

BICYCLE AND MOPED HIRE *(bicicletas/velomotores de alquiler)*

Bicycles can be hired in most resorts on a daily or weekly basis. Rates for mopeds are considerably higher. Insurance is obligatory and costs extra, and a deposit will also be required. A special motorbike permit is needed for machines of over 50cc, and the wearing of crash helmets is compulsory.

I'd like to hire a bicycle	**Quisiera alquilar una bicicleta**
What's the charge per day/week?	**¿Cuánto cobran por día/ semana?**

BUDGETING FOR YOUR TRIP

To enable you to estimate the cost of your holiday, here's a list of some average prices in euros. They can only be approximate, however, as prices vary from place to place, and inflation in Spain creeps up relentlessly. Prices quoted may be subject to IVA, at variable rates.

Accommodation: Rates for a double room can range from as low as €40 at a *pensión* or *hostal* to as much as €1,000 at a top-of-the-range, luxury 5-star hotel. As a rule of thumb, a nice 4-star hotel will cost between €100 and €150. Some hotels may have three or four pricing seasons. For example, in Sevilla during the Easter Week celebrations and the subsequent *Feria de Abril*, rates can be double what you would normally be charged.

Car hire: Prices vary dramatically depending on whether you hire before your trip starts, whether you hire from a company in your own country or locally, how long you hire for, whether you want an automatic or manual transmission vehicle, and what insurance coverage you want – or are obliged – to purchase.

If you want a small, manual transmission car primarily for local use, then it may be cheaper to rent from a local company on the Costa del Sol. However, for those wanting to be assured that a car is waiting for them on arrival, **Mondialautos**, www.mondialautos.com, offers extremely competitive rates.

Entertainment: A cinema ticket costs around €8, a flamenco nightclub (entry and first drink) starts at around €25, and a disco from €10. Amusement parks cost around €25 per adult or €18 per child per day. A bullfight ticket ranges from €30 to €135.

Meals and drinks: In a bar, a Continental breakfast will cost around €4. The cheapest three-course meal with one drink, a *menú del día* in a small bar or restaurant, will be around €10–12. Dinner in a moderately priced restaurant will be about €20–30 per person, including wine. At the top restaurants, expect to pay up to €60 or more per person, plus wine.

In a bar, a draught beer *(una caña)* or a small bottle will range from €2 to €2.50, a coffee around €1, a Spanish brandy from €1.50 to €2, a soft drink from €1.50 and a glass of local wine about €2. Sitting at an outside table usually means you pay more for a drink than if you sit inside at the bar.

Shopping: Again, prices can vary substantially. By far the cheapest places are the large hypermarkets such as Pryca where, for example, a can of San Miguel beer might cost around €0.75–1. In a small corner shop or *supermercado* (supermarket) the same beer might cost about €1 and similar price differentials exist for most other goods.

Sightseeing: Tickets to the major sights, such as Sevilla's Real Alcáza and Córdoba's Mezquita cost around €8; and the Alhambra in Granada €12. Admission prices for most museums, galleries, cathedrals, etc. are far more modest.

Sports: Per-day green fees for golf range from around €50 up to as much as €200 at the very top courses. Tennis court fees start at €8 per hour. Horse riding starts at about €15 per hour.

Taxis: Taxis are generally inexpensive, with a typical city-centre trip costing around €5. It's best to establish the rate for a long-distance journey before you depart. There are fixed rates, well displayed, for all destinations from Málaga's international airport (www.aena.es)

Train: The *cercanías* (local) line between Málaga and Fuengirola is a fast, clean and inexpensive way to travel along this part of the Costa del Sol. A return (round-trip) ticket costs €4.10, and a single ticket aboard the regional train from Málaga to Sevilla costs €18.15.

C

CAMPING

There are numerous official campsites along the Costa del Sol and throughout Andalucía. Facilities vary, but most have electricity and running water, and many have shops and children's playgrounds. Some even have launderettes and restaurants. Rates depend on the facilities available. For a complete list of campsites, consult the *Guía de Campings*, available from the Spanish National Tourist Office and some local bookshops.

Camping outside of official sites is permitted, provided you obtain permission from the landowner. However, you are not allowed to pitch your tent on tourist beaches, in urban areas, or within 1km (½ mile) of an official site.

May we camp here?   ¡Podemos acampar aquí?

CAR HIRE *(coches de alquiler;* see also DRIVING)

Unless you plan to stay in one of the remote parts of the Costa del Sol, or are touring extensively, a car is superfluous to your requirements. In fact, if you are based at one of the popular resorts or major cities, having a car is more of a disadvantage than an advantage (it's hard to find places to park and there's always the possibility that your car will be broken into).

However, if you do decide to hire a car there are numerous firms operating in the cities and resorts of the Costa del Sol but it's wise to shop around as daily rates can vary enormously. **Mondialautos** (www.mondialautos.com) offers an excellent selection of brand-new cars with fully comprehensive insurance, unlimited mileage, free changes and cancellations and telephone support in English, and has offices in many cities in Andalucía and Gibraltar. Reserving your car before you leave home is usually cheaper.

Comprehensive insurance coverage should be considered a necessity, even if it doesn't come as part of the package. Theft from cars is all too common in this region, and extra coverage against the theft of the radio and other car parts and damage caused by thieves is very reasonable and seriously worth considering.

Normally, you must be over 21 to hire a car and you will need a valid driving licence that you have held for at least 12 months, your passport and a major credit card – cash deposits are high and are not always accepted. Visitors from countries other than the US, Canada and those in the EU may be expected to present an International Driver's Licence.

I'd like to hire a car (tomorrow) for one day/a week	**Quisiera alquilar un coche (para mañana) por un día/una semana**
Please include full insurance coverage	**Haga el favor de incluir el seguro a todo riesgo**

CLIMATE

Plenty of hot sunshine and cloudless skies are the rule on the Costa del Sol, and in most parts of Andalucía, too. But there are seasonal variations worth noting when you choose your holiday. From June to September, very hot days with low humidity are followed by slightly cooler evenings; rain is a rarity. In April, May and October, daytime temperatures remain quite warm, but it can get cold at night. From November to March, sunshine can still be enjoyed, but may be interrupted by chill winds from the mountains and even rain – on average four to six rainy days a month in winter – so be prepared.

Inland, the climate is different. The triangle between Sevilla, Córdoba and Granada is the hottest in Europe, with summertime temperatures often well over 40°C (104°F). As their name suggests, the Sierra Nevada Mountains near Granada see snow in the winter.

The average monthly temperatures for Málaga are:

	J	F	M	A	M	J	J	A	S	O	N	D
max°C	16	17	19	21	23	27	29	29	28	23	19	17
min°C	8	8	10	12	14	17	20	21	19	15	11	8
max°F	60	62	66	70	73	80	83	83	79	73	66	62
min°F	46	46	50	54	57	62	68	69	67	60	53	46
sea °C	15	14	15	16	17	21	21	23	21	18	17	14
°F	59	57	59	60	62	69	69	73	69	65	62	57

CLOTHING

From June to September the days are always hot and lightweight cotton clothes are the order of the day. During the rest of the year, a light jacket and a raincoat or umbrella will come in handy. Warmer attire will be needed in Granada and the Sierra Nevada during the winter. Respectable (i.e. modest) clothing should, of course, be worn when visiting churches, although women are no longer expected to cover their heads.

COMPLAINTS

By law, all hotels and restaurants must have official complaint forms (*hojas de reclamaciones*) and produce them on demand. The original of this triplicate document should be sent to the Ministry of Tourism; one copy remains with the establishment involved and one copy is given to you. The very act of asking for the *hoja* may resolve the problem in itself, as the establishment knows that tourism authorities take a serious view of such complaints.

CRIME AND SAFETY

Spain's crime rate is similar to that of other Western European countries, so the usual precautions apply. All thefts must be reported to the police within 24 hours and you will need a copy of the police report in order to make a claim on your insurance.

It's a good idea to photocopy the relevant pages of your passport and airline ticket and keep them in a separate place from the originals. If your passport is stolen, your consulate should be informed (*see* EMBASSIES AND CONSULATES).

I want to report a theft.	**Quiero denunciar un robo.**
My handbag/ticket/wallet/ passport has been stolen	**Me han robado el bolso/el billete/ la cartera/el pasaporte.**
Help! Thief!	**¡Socorro! ¡Ladrón!**

CUSTOMS *(aduana)* AND ENTRY REQUIREMENTS

Most visitors, including citizens of EU countries, the US, Canada, Ireland, Australia and New Zealand require only a valid passport – no visa, no health certificate – to enter Spain. Visitors from South Africa, however, must have a visa.

Currency restrictions: Tourists are allowed to bring an unlimited amount of euros or foreign currency into the country. On departure you must declare any amount beyond the equivalent of €6,000.

D

DRIVING

Drive on the right, overtake on the left. Give way to traffic coming from the right.

Road conditions: The old main road along the Costa del Sol, the N340, has been almost entirely superseded by a motorway, the A7, which runs from Algeciras almost to Almuñecar on the Costa Tropical and from Adra to Almeria. The missing section in the middle is being completed in stages and will join the motorway from Granada to Motril. West of Málaga the coastal motorway can be very busy and there is a toll-paying alternative, the AP7. Other motorways link Málaga with Seville, Córdoba and Granada and Algeciras with Seville, Jerez de la Frontera and Cádiz.

Main ('N') roads in Andalucía are generally fast and good. In general, Andalucía is a mountainous region and there are long, winding stretches of road where it is essential to drive slowly. A few less frequented backroads are in bad state of repair. Signposting is of variable quality but the usual way to find your way around in Spain is to ask the locals.

Entering Gibraltar by car: If you arrive by car (Gibraltar is less than two hours' drive from Málaga), you have two choices, neither of which is ideal. It is easier and often much faster to leave your car in one of the car parks in La Línea and cross the border on foot. Once you are in Gibraltar, a car is a hindrance in the town centre and only really useful if you want to take a tour of the Upper Rock. However, the downside of this strategy is the risk of having your car broken into in La Línea. If you want to take your vehicle with you, bear in mind that there may be long delays in either direction. Beyond the customs area, access to Gibraltar is across the middle of the airport runway (the road has to be closed when aircraft land and take off), then past the defensive walls to the town centre.

Rules and regulations: Speed limits are 50kph (30mph) in built-up areas, 90–100kph (55–60mph) on highways and 120kph (75mph) on motorways. A reflective yellow jacket for roadside emergencies must be carried in the passenger compartment of the vehicle. The use of seat belts (front and back seats) is obligatory. A red warning triangle must be carried. Motorcycle riders and their passengers must wear crash helmets. Spanish roads are patrolled by the motorcycle police of the *Guardia Civil*. They can impose on-the-spot fines for common offences including speeding, travelling too close to the car in front and driving with burned-out lights.

Fuel: Service stations are plentiful, but it's a good idea to keep an eye on the gauge in more remote areas, like the Alpujarras.

Parking *(aparcamiento)*: Parking regulations are strictly en-

Full tank, please, top grade.	**Llénelo, por favor, con super.**
Please check the oil/ tyres/battery.	**Por favor, controle el aceite/ los neumáticos/la batería.**

forced – offending vehicles will be towed away and a hefty fine charged for their return. A yellow-painted kerb means parking is prohibited at all times; blue means you must pay for a ticket at the meter to be displayed in your car.

If you need help: The Civil Guard is efficient with minor mechanical problems and go out of their way to help you if you have a breakdown. Spanish garages *(talleres)* are also efficient, but in tourist areas major repairs may take several days because of heavy workload. Spare parts are readily available for most major makes of cars.

There's been an accident.	**Ha habido un accidente.**
My car has broken down.	**Mi coche se ha estropeado**
Where is the nearest garage?	**¿Donde está el garage más cercano?**

Road signs: Most of the road signs used in Spain are international pictograms. But here are some written signs you will come across:

autopista (de peaje)	(toll) motorway (expressway)
ceda el paso	give way
circunvalación	bypass/ring-road
curva peligrosa	dangerous bend
despacio	slow
desviación	diversion
obras	road works
peligro	danger
prohibido aparcar	no parking
salida de camiones	truck exit
sin plomo	unleaded petrol
Can I park here?	**¿Se puede aparcar aquí?**

E

ELECTRICITY *(corriente eléctrica)*

220v/50Hz AC is now standard. An adapter for Continental-style two-pin sockets will be needed.

EMBASSIES AND CONSULATES *(embajadas y consulados)*

Australia: Federico Rubio 14, 41004 Sevilla, tel: 954 220 971.
Canada: Plata de la Malagueta, 3, 29017 Málaga, tel: 952 223 346.
Republic of Ireland: Avenida de los Boliches 15, 29640 Fuengirola, tel: 952 475 108. Plaza de Santa Cruz, 6-Baja, Sevilla, tel: 954 216 361.
UK: Mauricio Moro Pareto, 2, Edificio Eurocom Bloque Sur, 29006 Málaga, tel: 952 352 300.
US: Centro Comercial Las Rampas II, 29640 Fuengirola, tel: 952 474 891. Paseo de Las Delicias 7, 41012 Sevilla, tel: 954 231 885.

EMERGENCIES *(emergencias)*

Unless you are fluent in Spanish, you should seek help through your hotel receptionist or the local tourist office. If you can speak Spanish, the following telephone numbers may be useful:

	Ambulance	Police	Sea Rescue
Spain	112	091	900202202
Gibraltar	112	199	

G

GETTING THERE (see also AIRPORTS)

By Air

Spain's national carrier is Iberia (www.iberia.com) which has direct flights from London to the main Andalusian cities. British Airways (www.ba.com) has flights from London to Málaga and Gibraltar. The best fares, however, are always to be had by shopping around on line between the many cut-price airlines which now operate routes between various London and regional UK airports. These include BMI Baby (www.bmibaby.com), Easy Jet (www.easyjet.com), Monarch (www.flymonarch.com) and Ryanair (www.ryanair.com). There are also many package holiday charter flights from Britain to Málaga which roll transport and hotel accommodation into one price – if you buy at the last minute you may get a good deal.

By Road

From the UK, the main route from the French ferry ports runs south through western France to Bordeaux and into Spain at Irún, west of the Pyrenees. Continue on the A8 to San Sebastián and from there take the N1 to Vitoria-Gasteiz, the AP7 to Burgos and the A1/E5 all the way to Madrid. Go around Madrid on the M50 and then take the A4/E5 south to Bailén. From there, continue on the A4/E5 westwards to Córdoba and Sevilla and then on the AP4/E5 to Cádiz via Jerez de la Frontera; or from Bailén take the A44 south via Jaén to Granada then go south to the coast at Motril. From Granada you can take the A92 and A45 to reach Málaga.

Alternatively, take the route through central France to Perpignan and follow the A7 motorway south via Barcelona, Tarragona, Valencia and Alicante to Murcia. From Murcia continue to Puerto Lumbreras and take the A7/E15 to Almería and Málaga.

Your driving time (three steady days by either route) can be cut by using the long-distance car-ferry service from Plymouth to Santander or Portsmouth to Bilbao in northern Spain *(see page 118)*. From Santander or Bilbao, follow the road to Burgos and proceed as above.

By Rail

The best way to get to Spain by train from the UK is to take the high-speed Eurostar service (www.eurostar.com) from London St Pancras to Paris Gare du Nord. Cross the city to the Paris Austerlitz and catch the Elipsos 'Francisco de Goya' overnight train (trenhotel, www.elipsos.com) via Poitiers, Vitoria-Gazteiz, Burgos and Valladolid to Madrid. In Madrid you need to change stations again from Chamartin to Atocha to catch the train to Málaga or any other major city in Andalucía. The whole journey takes about 20 hours.

The alternative is to catch a SNCF train (www.sncf.com) from Paris to the Hendaye-Irun on the southwest Franco-Spanish frontier and here take a Spanish train (www.renfe.es) to Madrid. This route is slower and less direct.

A third option is to take the Joan Miró trenhotel from Paris to Barcelona and proceed to Madrid and Andalucía from there.

Other international trenhotel services are between Milan and Barcelona (Salvador Dalí) and Zurich and Barcelona (Pau Casals).

International rail tickets can be booked through Rail Europe (www.raileurope.com); another useful source of rail information is www.seat61.com.

By Sea

From the UK, two companies offer car-ferry services to mainland Spain, with timetables varying by the season. Brittany Ferries (tel: 0871 244 0744, www.brittany-ferries.com) has sailings between Plymouth and Santander (average crossing time 24 hours). P&O European Ferries (tel: 0871 664 5645, www.poferries.com) has sailings between Portsmouth and Bilbao (average crossing time 35 hours). Motorists can then drive from Santander or Bilbao to Burgos and then continue south, using the directions in the BY ROAD section *on page 116*, to the Costa del Sol and Andalucía.

GUIDES AND TOURS

English-speaking guides can be hired through local tourist offices (*see* TOURIST INFORMATION *on page 128*). Guided tours and excursions can be booked at most hotels or through any of the numerous travel agencies *(agencia de viaje)*.

H

HEALTH AND MEDICAL CARE

Anything other than basic emergency treatment can be very expensive and you should not leave home without adequate insurance, preferably including coverage for an emergency flight home in the event of serious injury or illness.

EU citizens are entitled to free emergency hospital treatment. Britons need a European Health Insurance Card (tel: 0845 606 2030, www.ehic.org, or application form from the post office). You may have to pay all or part of the price of treatment and medicines; keep receipts to claim a refund when you return home.

The main health hazard on the Costa del Sol is also its biggest attraction – the sun. Take a sun hat, sunglasses and high-factor sunscreen, cover up between noon and 4pm and limit sunbathing to an hour or less until you begin to tan. Children under 3 years have very delicate skin and should not be exposed to the sun at all. For minor ailments, visit the local first-aid post *(ambulatorio)*. Away from your hotel, don't hesitate to ask the police or a tourist information office for help. At your hotel, ask the staff for assistance. *Farmacias* (chemists) are usually open during normal shopping hours. After hours, at least one *farmacia* in every town remains open all night. Called a *farmacia de guardia*, its location is posted in the window of all other *farmacias* and in the local newspapers.

Where's the nearest (all-night) chemist?	**¿Dónde está la farmacia (de guardia) más cercana?**
I need a doctor/dentist	**Necesito un médico/dentista**
I feel unwell	**Me siento mal**
It hurts here	**Me duele aquí**
I have a temperature	**Tengo fiebre**
sunburn/sunstroke	**quemadura del sol/ una insolación**
an upset stomach	**molestias de estómago**

HOLIDAYS *(días festivos)*

Andalucía celebrates its regional holiday on 28 February, and banks, post offices, government offices and many other businesses are also closed on the following dates. Note that there are a number of local and regional holidays and saints' days too; check with the local tourist office.

1 January	*Año Nuevo*	New Year's Day
6 January	*Epifanía*	Epiphany
19 March	*San José*	St Joseph's Day
1 May	*Día del Trabajo*	Labour Day
25 July	*Santiago Apóstol*	St James's Day
15 August	*Asunción*	Assumption Day
12 October	*Día de la Hispanidad*	Columbus Day

1 November	*Todos los Santos*	All Saints' Day
6 December	*Día de la Constitución*	Constitution Day
8 December	*Inmaculada Concepción*	Immaculate Conception
25 December	*Día de Navidad*	Christmas Day

Moveable dates:

Jueves Santo	Maundy Thursday; late March–mid-April
Viernes Santo	Good Friday; late March–mid-April
Corpus Cristi	mid-June

L

LANGUAGE

The national language of Spain, Castilian, is spoken in the Costa del Sol and Andalucía. Throughout Andalucía, the local variation, Andaluz, which is a little more difficult to understand, is commonly used. English is widely spoken in the resort towns, though it is helpful to learn at least a few basic phrases in Castilian. The *Berlitz Spanish Phrasebook and Dictionary* covers most situations you are likely to encounter, and the *Berlitz Spanish-English/English-Spanish Pocket Dictionary* contains some 12,500 entries, plus a menu-reader supplement.

M

MEDIA (see also WEBSITES)

Radio and television *(radio; televisión)*: There are several radio stations that broadcast in English on the FM band, such as REM.FM (91.9 and 104.8), Central FM (98.6 and 103.8), Spectrum FM (105.5) and on the Costa Almería/Mojácar (92.6). Radio broadcasts can also be picked up from Gibraltar. Network television programmes are all in Spanish, but the more expensive hotels and many British bars also have satellite TV with CNN, MTV, BBC, Sky TV etc.

Newspapers and magazines *(periódicos, revistas)*: In the major tourist areas you can buy most European newspapers on the day of publication. The *International Herald Tribune* is also widely available as are all kinds of British and American magazines. The weekly *Sur in English*, available free, is aimed at residents on the Costa del Sol and carries local news and events. Other English language magazines and newspapers are published in different parts of the coast serving expatriate communities.

MONEY

Currency: The euro (EUR) is the official currency used in Spain. Notes are denominated in 5, 10, 20, 50, 100 and 500 euros; coins in 1 and 2 euros and 1, 2, 5, 10, 20 and 50 cents.

Currency exchange: Outside of normal banking hours, many travel agencies and other businesses displaying a *cambio* sign will change foreign currency into euros. Larger hotels will also change guests' money. The exchange rate is slightly worse than at the bank. Travellers cheques always get a better rate than cash. Take your passport when changing money or travellers' cheques, for identification purposes.

I want to change some pounds/dollars	**Quiero cambiar libras/dólares**
Do you accept travellers cheques?	**¿Acepta usted cheques de viajes?**
Can I pay with this credit card?	**¿Puedo pagar con esta tarjeta de crédito?**

ATMs: ATMs *(cajeros automáticos)* can be found almost everywhere, and from them you can draw funds in euros against your bank account with a credit or debit card.

Credit cards: All the internationally recognised cards are accepted by most hotels, restaurants and businesses in Spain.

VAT *(IVA)*: Remember that IVA *(impuesto sobre el valor agregado)*, the Spanish equivalent of value-added tax, will be added to your hotel and restaurant bills; it currently stands at 7 percent. A higher rate of 16 percent applies to car-hire charges and a rate of 4 percent applies to certain basic necessities.

O

OPENING HOURS

Shops and offices and other businesses generally observe the afternoon siesta, opening 9am–1.30 or 2pm, and 4.30 or 5pm–7.30 or 8pm, but in tourist areas many places now stay open all day. Banks are generally open 9am–2pm, but will, of course, be closed on the numerous public holidays.

P

POLICE *(policía)*

There are three separate police forces in Spain. The *Policía Municipal*, who are attached to the local town hall and usually wear blue uniforms, are the ones to whom you should report theft and other crimes. The *Policía Nacional* is the national anti-crime unit wearing dark-blue uniforms; and the *Guardia Civil*, with green uniforms, is a national force with both military and civilian functions whose most conspicuous role is as a highway patrol. Spanish police officers are generally courteous and helpful towards foreign visitors.

The emergency number is **912**.

POST OFFICES *(correos)*

Post offices handle mail and telegrams only; normally, you cannot make telephone calls from them. Routine postal business is generally transacted 8.30am–2.30pm Mon–Fri, and 9.30am–1pm Sat. Postage stamps *(sellos)* can also be bought at tobacconists *(estancos)*, at hotel desks and at tourist shops selling postcards. Mail for destinations outside Spain should be posted in the yellow boxes marked *extranjero* (overseas); delivery is slow.

PUBLIC TRANSPORT

By Bus *(autobús)*: Buses are an excellent form of transport, not just along the Costa del Sol but throughout Andalucía. They reach many destinations that the train doesn't, and when they do serve the same places, they are often cheaper, faster and more frequent. Portillo (www.ctsa-portillo.com) operates a service every half-hour from Málaga that connects Torremolinos, Benalmádena-Costa, Fuengirola, Marbella, San Pedro Alcántara and Estepona. Alsina Graells Sur (www.alsa.es) operates daily services between Málaga and Sevilla, Granada, Córdoba, Almería and La Linea de la Concepción, a short walk from the border with Gibraltar.

Where is the (nearest) bus stop?	**¿Dónde está la parada de autobuses (más cercana)?**
When's the next bus/ boat for…?	**¿A qué hora sale el próximo autobús/barco para…?**
I want a ticket to…	**Quiero un billete para…**
single (one-way)	**ida**
return (round-trip)	**ida y vuelta**
Will you tell me when to get off?	**¿Podría indicarme cuándo tengo que bajar?**

By Ferry *(barco)*: Algeciras is a major port and Trasmediterránea (tel: 902 454 645, www.trasmediterranea.com) is the largest company operating from there. It has frequent sailings, on high-speed or regular ferries, to Ceuta, a Spanish enclave on the Moroccan coast, or Tangier, Morocco. It also operates a daily ferry on the much longer routes from Málaga (no service Friday) and Almería to Melilla, the other Spanish enclave on the Moroccan coast. There is also a very limited ferry service operating between Gibraltar and Tangier.

By Taxi *(taxi)*: Taxis in the major cities have meters, but in villages along the rest of the coast they usually don't, so it's a good idea to check the fare before you get in. If you take a long trip, you will be charged a two-way fare whether you make the return journey or not. By law a taxi may carry only four people. A green light and/or a *libre* (free) sign indicates that a taxi is available. You can telephone for a cab as well. The numbers to call are as follows: in Benalmádena, tel: 952 441 545; in Estepona, tel: 952 802 900; in Fuengirola, tel: 951 471 000; in Málaga, tel: 952 327 950; in Marbella, tel: 952 783 950; in Torremolinos, tel: 952 380 600; and in Gibraltar, tel: 20070027.

By Train *(tren)*: A suburban *(cercanías)* rail service runs along the coast between central Málaga (Maria Zambrano station) and Fuengirola. It includes stops at the RENFE train station, the international airport in Málaga, Torremolinos and Benalmádena. Trains depart from Málaga every 30 minutes between 5.19am and 10.19pm. From Fuengirola, there is half-hourly service between 6.09am and 11.09pm.

From the mainline (RENFE) station in Málaga there are services to Ronda, Córdoba, Granada and Sevilla, from where there are connections to other destinations in Andalucía. One of Europe's most scenic short rail journeys is the 80km (50-mile), single-track stretch between Algeciras and Ronda, which climbs steeply through the mountains. There are also long-distance *(largo recorrido)* trains via Córdoba to Madrid and Barcelona. Timetables and information are available from railway stations and tourist offices. RENFE has one information number, tel: 902 240 202, plus its website www.renfe.es.

Train Passes: For information on rail passes and tickets on Spanish trains, including the high-speed Euromed (Barcelona, Valencia, Alicante) or AVE (Madrid, Córdoba, Sevilla, Cádiz, Málaga) trains, American visitors should contact Rail Europe (tel: 800-622-8600, www.raileurope.com), *before* leaving for Europe; in the UK, contact Rail Europe (tel: 08448 484 064, www.raileurope.co.uk).

If you are resident in a qualifying European country you can get a single-country pass valid for 3 to 8 days within a month. Prices are from £100 to £212. Alternatively you can buy a multi-country Interrail pass valid for 30 participating European countries including Spain. US visitors will need to apply for a Eurail pass which gives unlimited first or second class travel for 3 to 10 days within a specified two month period. Adult prices vary from $205 to $526 depending on the class and the days.

R

RELIGION

Spain is a predominantly Roman Catholic country. Bilingual mass in English/Spanish is conducted at the Church of Virgen del Carmen (Avda. Bonanza) in Benalmádena-Costa every Sunday at 10am and at St Andrew's Chapel (Edificio Jupiter, Avenida Jesús Santos Rein) in Los Boliches every Saturday at 11.30pm. Anglicans can attend St George's Church in the British Cemetery (400m east of the bullring), where Holy Communion is held every Sunday at 11am, Other Protestant denominations such as the Church of Scotland (Presbyterian) and the Methodist church are represented on the Costa del Sol. In addition, there are congregations of Christian Scientists, Jehovah's Witnesses and Mormons here. Muslim mosques can be found in Málaga, Fuengirola and Marbella, and there are a number of synagogues in Marbella and Torremolinos. For full details of services, refer to *Sur in English*, www.surinenglish.com/service/church-services, or contact the local tourist office.

T

TELEPHONE *(teléfono)*

The country code for Spain is 34. To obtain information from Spain, dial 11825.

In addition to the telephone office, *Telefónica*, in Málaga and other major towns and cities, there are phone booths everywhere from which you can make local and international calls. Instructions in English and area codes for different countries are displayed in the booths. International calls are expensive, so be sure to have a plentiful supply of suitable euro coins. Some telephones accept credit cards, and many require a phone card *(tarjeta telefónica)*, available from a tobacconist and some shops where you will see a sign outside. To call overseas, pick up the receiver, wait for the dial tone, then dial 00. Wait for a second tone, then dial the country code, area code (minus the initial zero) and number.

Remember, calling directly from your hotel room is almost always prohibitively expensive unless you are using a calling card. Very cheap telephone rates are available from Internet cafés and shops displaying a *Locutorio* sign.

Can you get me this number?	¿Puede comunicarme con este número?

TIME DIFFERENCES

Spanish time coincides with most of Western Europe – Greenwich Mean Time plus one hour. In summer, another hour is added for daylight saving time.

New York	London	**Spain**	Sydney	Auckland
6am	11am	**noon**	8pm	10pm

TIPPING

Since a service charge is normally included in hotel and restaurant bills, tipping is not obligatory, but 10 percent can be added if service was exceptional. About 10 percent of the bill is usual for taxi drivers and hairdressers and others offering personal services. In a bar it is customary to leave some small change to round up the bill.

TOILETS

There are many expressions for toilets in Spanish: *aseos, servicios, baños, sanitarios,* WC and *retretes*; the first two are the most common. Just about every bar and restaurant has a toilet available for public use, but it is polite to buy a drink in the bar if you are going in there just to use the facilities. The usual signs are *Damas* for women and *Caballeros* for men, though you might also see *Señoras* and *Señores*.

TOURIST INFORMATION OFFICES *(oficinas de turismo)*

To assist you in planning your holiday, a great deal of information can be obtained from one of the international branches of the Spanish National Tourist Office, as listed below.

Canada: 2 Bloor Street West, 34th Floor, Toronto, Ontario M4W 3E2, tel: 416-961-3131, fax: 416-961-1992, e-mail: toronto@tourspain.es.
UK: 2nd Floor, 79 New Cavendish Street, London W1W 6XB, tel: 020 7317 2010, fax: 020 7317 2048, e-mail: londres@tourspain.es.
US: Water Tower Place, Suite 915 East, 845 North Michigan Avenue, Chicago, IL 60611, tel: 312 642 1992, fax: 312 642 9817, e-mail: chicago@tourspain.es.
8383 Wilshire Boulevard, Suite 960, Beverly Hills, Los Angeles, CA 90211, tel: 323 658 7195, fax: 323 658 1061, e-mail: losangeles@tourspain.es.

665 Fifth Avenue, New York, NY 10103, tel: 212 265 8822, fax: 212 265 8864, e-mail: nuevayork@tourspain.es.
1395 Brickell Avenue, Miami, FL 33131, tel: 305 358 1992, fax: 305 358 8223, e-mail: miami@tourspain.es.

For more detailed information about the Costa del Sol, contact the Costa del Sol Patronato de Turismo, Plaza del Siglo, 2, 29015 Málaga, tel: 952 126 272, www.visitcostadelsol.com.

For more detailed information about Gibraltar, contact the Gibraltar Information Bureau, Duke of Kent House, Cathedral Square, tel: (350) 200 450 00, www.gibraltar.gov.gi.

For information about Andalucía, contact Turismo Andaluz, Compañía 40, tel: 952 129 300, www.andalucia.org.

For more information about individual cities and towns, visit the local tourist office *(oficina de turismo)*. Offices are normally open 9am–1pm and 4–7pm, and all of them have somebody on staff who will be able to give advice in English. Major offices are located in the following cities: Granada, tel: 958 223 527; Sevilla, tel: 954 221 404; Málaga, tel: 952 213 445; Marbella, tel: 952 771 442.

V

VAT REFUNDS

The Spanish Government levies a value-added tax (called IVA) on most items in shops. Tourists from outside the EU who spend a minimum of €100 in stores where there is a 'tax free' shopping logo can claim a refund of the IVA they pay. When you make your purchase, ask the shop for a tax-free receipt. You will have to show your passport. At customs on departure (within three months of purchase), show the goods you have bought and get the tax-free receipt stamped. Claim the amount of tax paid from one of the companies authorised to process VAT returns – they have branches at all airports. You can ask to be refunded in cash but the easiest way is for the amount to be added to your credit card account.

W

WEBSITES (see also ACCOMMODATION, GETTING THERE, PUBLIC TRANSPORT and TOURIST INFORMATION)

For general tourist information, look at:
www.spain.info Spanish National Tourist Office site
www.visitcostadelsol.com Costa del Sol Tourist Office site
www.andalucia.org Andalucía site
www.malagaturismo.com site for Málaga
www.marbella.es/turismo site for Marbella
www.gibraltar.gov.gi site for Gibraltar
www.granadatur.com site for Granada
www.turismodecordoba.org site for Córdoba
www.turismo.sevilla.org site for Sevilla

You could also try:
www.webmalaga.com
www.costasol.com
www.legadoandalusi.es an organisation marking routes around Andalucía, in Spanish

The English-language publications *Sur in English* and *Costa del Sol News* have websites that have information about special events. Check out: **www.surinenglish.com** and **costa-news.com**.

Y

YOUTH HOSTELS (*albergues de juveniles;* see also ACCOMMODATION, CAMPING and WEBSITES)

Red de Albergues Juveniles de Andalucía provides a complete listing of all youth hostels on the Costa del Sol and in Andalucía on their website www.inturjoven.com. Note that the Spanish word *hostal* does not mean youth hostel, but a basic hotel.

Recommended Hotels

These hotels in the Costa del Sol and Andalucía are listed alphabetically by region or town. For each one we give its Spanish hotel grade (*explained in Accommodation on page 105*) and its price category. Wheelchair accessibility is not common in Spain. Although one or two smaller hotels may cater to people with disabilities, it is generally the larger and more expensive places that have such facilities. As a basic guide we have used the symbols below to indicate prices per night for a double room with bath or shower, including service charge and taxes, during the high season. Low-season rates can be considerably lower. Please note that these rates do not include breakfast. All these hotels accept major credit cards unless stated otherwise.

€€€€€	180–300 euros and over
€€€€	120–180 euros
€€€	90–120 euros
€€	60–90 euros
€	below 60 euros

CADIZ

Hotel Monte Puertatierra (4 stars) €€€ *Avenida de Andalucía 34, tel: 956 272 111, fax: 956 250 311, www.hotelesmonte.com.* Beautifully designed modern hotel with a fine location, close to both the beach and old town. All expected amenities including on-site parking. 98 rooms.

CARMONA

Casa de Carmona (5 stars) €€€€ *Plaza de Lasso 1, tel: 954 191 000, fax: 954 190 189, www.casadecarmona.com.* A 16th-century Renaissance palace carefully and lovingly renovated into a beautiful and very hospitable luxury hotel, featuring a finely proportioned inner courtyard, airy breakfast terrace and the elegant Gracia Real restaurant. Every room is individually decorated and filled with handpicked antiques from Madrid, London and Paris. 33 rooms.

Cortijo El Triguero €€ *Carretera N-398 Carmona–El Viso del Alcor, Km18, tel: 955 953 626, www.eltriguero.com.* Found way off the road, just a short distance from Carmona, this is a beautiful farmhouse surrounded by fields and a fighting-bull ranch. Expect traditional décor, a tranquil environment, good but unobtrusive service and a nice pool. 9 rooms.

CÓRDOBA

Hotel Casa de los Azulejos (3 stars) €€€–€€€€ *Fernando Colón 5, tel: 957 470 000, www.casadelosazulejos.com.* A 17th-century house, renovated in a Sevillana style, the Azulejos has a very interesting atmosphere. All rooms are set around a courtyard. Traditional décor, a formal restaurant and the more laid-back Guadalupana Cantina with Mariachi singers on Saturday lunchtime. 8 rooms.

Hotel Macía Alfaros (4 stars) €€€ *Alfaros 18, tel: 957 491 920, fax: 957 492 210, www.maciahoteles.com.* Just a short walk from the Mezquita, this is a dignified oasis of calm in the old quarter. Moorish in style, it has elegant rooms, a pool, restaurants and private parking. 144 rooms.

Hotel Palacio del Baílio (5 stars) €€€€€ *Ramírez de las Casas Deza 10–12, tel: 957 498 993, fax: 957 498 994, www.hospes.es.* This palace, built over the ruins of a Roman house, was originally erected after the Reconquest in Córdoba. It also features stables, coach houses, lofts, granaries, Roman remains, valuable art and a grand garden, all of which have now been transformed into a beautiful hotel with totally modern facilities. 48 rooms, 5 suites.

ESTEPONA

Alsatli Spa Hotel (4 stars) €€€€–€€€€€ *Carretera 340, Km166.5, tel: 952 889 043, fax: 952 887 060, www.alsatlispa hotel.com.* Large spa hotel on the 'Golden Mile' between Marbella and Estepona, with an attractive combination of the modern and the traditional. Located right on the beach, it has a gastronomic restaurant, six swimming pools and Jacuzzi as well as the pleasing spa. 180 rooms.

Kempinski Hotel Bahía Estepona (5 stars) €€€€€ *Carretera de Cádiz, Km159, tel: 952 809 500, fax: 952 809 550, www.kempinski- spain.com.* The rooms in this architecturally interesting hotel all have sea views. There are also subtropical gardens, a 1-km (½-mile) beach, numerous swimming pools, water sports, horse-riding and a restaurant serving haute cuisine. 147 rooms.

Las Dunas Beach Hotel & Spa (5 stars GL) €€€€€ *Urb. La Bobadilla Baja, Carretera Cádiz, Km163.5, tel: 952 809 400, fax: 952 809 406, www.las-dunas.com.* A low-rise Andalusian-style *hacienda* with Moorish influences. Soothing colour schemes inside and out; sub-tropical gardens leading to the beach; sports and health club. Luxurious rooms with terraces or sun decks offering marvellous views. 73 rooms.

FUENGIROLA

Hotel Beatriz Palace & Spa (4 stars) €€€€ *A7, Km207, tel: 952 922 000, fax: 952 922 005, www.beatrizhoteles.com.* Found just south of the castle, right on the beach, this is Fuengirola's newest and best-located hotel. It also has a very pleasing atmosphere, a variety of pools and spa facilities. 285 rooms, 6 suites.

GIBRALTAR

Caleta Hotel (4 stars) €€€€–€€€€€ *Catalan Bay, tel: 350 200 76501, fax: 350 20042143, www.caletahotel.com.* This hotel has the most dramatic location in Gibraltar, directly under the rock and overlooking the peaceful Catalan Bay on the least crowded side of Gibraltar. Be sure to request one of the rooms with a delightful sea view. 160 rooms.

GRANADA

Al Andalus Apartments €€–€€€ *Santa Ana 16, tel: 958 222 428, www.granada-in.com.* This group, which also operates the Hammam Baños Arabes, offers apartments in the historical areas of Granada for 2–8 people. The prices are very competitive, but at certain very busy times there are minimum stays of 3–5 nights.

Room Mate Los Migueletes (3 stars) €€€€–€€€€€ *Benalua 11, tel: 958 210 700, fax: 958 210 702, www.casamigueletes.com.* Located close to the Plaza Nueva, this is a beautiful 17th-century mansion complete with patios and galleries, and all the rooms are individually decorated. The hotel is a 'no smoking' area; parking is at the Plaza Puerta Real garage. 23 rooms and 2 suites.

Hotel Guadalupe (3 stars) €€–€€€ *Paseo de la Sabica S/N, tel: 958 223 423, fax: 958 223 798.* Situated in the Alhambra complex very close to the palace, this is a comfortable hotel with a Granadino- style atmosphere. 58 rooms.

Hotel Palacio de los Navas (3 stars) €€€€ *Navas 1, tel/fax: 958 215 760, www.palaciodelosnavas.com.* Dating from the 16th century, this building retains many original architectural features and is a charming hotel with a delightful mix of old and new located in the heart of Granada. 17 rooms, 2 suites.

Hotel Palacio de los Patos (5 stars) €€€€€ *Solarillo de Gracia 1, tel: 958 536 516, fax: 958 536 517, www.hospes.es.* A large, classical, 19th-century palace right on busy shopping street in the heart of the city. The interior décor features a graceful and intriguing combination of the old and the very new. With its Senzone Gastronomic Restaurant and Bodyna Spa & Sensations, this is *the* luxury hotel in Granada. 32 rooms, 10 suites.

GUILLENA

Hotel Cortijo Águila Real (4 stars) €€€–€€€€ *Carretera de Guillena– Burguillos, Km4, tel: 955 785 006, fax: 955 784 330, www.aguilareal.com.* A traditional farm, just 24km (15 miles) from the centre of Sevilla. Beautifully converted rooms around the main yard, fine restaurant, inviting pool and a small bullring. 8 rooms, 5 suites.

JEREZ DE LA FRONTERA

Hotel Los Jándalos Jerez (3 stars) €€€ *Nuño de Cañas 1, tel: 956 327 230, fax: 956 326 030, www.jandalos.com.* This stylish building, found between the Plaza de Toros and Avenida Alvaro Domecq, has uniquely decorated rooms, and a very colourful spa/hydrotherapy centre. 42 rooms and 17 duplexes.

Bellas Artes (4 stars) €€€€ *Plaza del Arroyo 45, tel: 956 348 430, www.hotelbellasartes.com.* A renovated mansion with individually styled rooms in the city centre near the cathedral and handily located for visiting other sights. Private car park. Other facilities include a bar/cafeteria and a library. 19 rooms, two junior suites and one suite.

Hotel Villa Jerez (5 stars) €€€€–€€€€€ *Avenida de la Cruz Roja 7, tel: 956 153 100, fax: 956 304 300, www.hace.es.* Set in its own pleasant gardens, this charming hotel offers an intriguing mix of traditional style and modern facilities. All of the rooms look out over either the pool or the garden, and the Las Yucas Restaurant offers fine regional and international cuisine. 18 rooms.

LOJA

La Bobadilla (5 stars GL) €€€€€ *Finca La Bobadilla, Apdo 144, tel: 958 321 861, fax: 958 321 810, www.barcelo.com.* Set within its own large grounds, this complex, designed to be a replica of an Arab village, is one of the most luxurious hotels in Europe. Found between Sevilla, Granada, Málaga and Córdoba, the huge rooms are stunning, and there is a gourmet restaurant, indoor and outdoor pools and even a private chapel where you can get married. 26 rooms, 34 junior suites, 6 suites, 3 imperial suites.

MÁLAGA

Hotel Don Curro (3 stars) €€€–€€€€ *Sancha de Lara 7, tel: 952 227 200, fax: 952 215 946, www.hoteldoncurro.com.* Well established hotel on a quiet side street right in the centre of the city. The rooms have a pleasing mix of modern and traditional décor and all modern facilities. Good value for money. 118 rooms.

Hotel Larios (4 stars) €€€–€€€€ *Marques de Larios 2, tel: 952 222 200, fax: 952 222 407, www.room-matehotels.com.* The Larios has an enviable position at the heart of Málaga's principal pedestrian shopping street, adjacent to the charming Plaza del Constitución. Unique in Málaga, the public areas and rooms have a delightful Art Deco design. Don't overlook either the rooftop *terraza*, where you can enjoy the best views over the city. 41 rooms.

Novotel Málaga Aeropuerto (4 stars) €€€ *Avenida de Velaquez 126, tel: 952 248 150, fax: 952 230 232, www.novotel.com*. This is a new hotel with a strategic location to the west of the city centre, right by the motorway that leads to all directions. With extra-large rooms, a good restaurant, and outdoor pool, this is also the nicest hotel that's close to the airport – just minutes away. 155 rooms.

Parador Málaga-Gibralfaro (4 stars) €€€€ *Castillo de Gibralfaro S/N, tel: 952 221 902, fax: 952 221 904, www.parador.es*. A small *parador*-grade hotel beside the Moorish castle on the hilltop above the city. Grand views over the city and the bay. 38 rooms.

MARBELLA

Don Carlos Beach & Golf Resort Hotel (5 stars) €€€€€ *Carretera de Cádiz, Km192, tel: 952 768 800, fax: 952 833 429, www.hoteldoncarlos.com*. Luxury hotel set in sub-tropical gardens on one of the best beaches on the coast, with views of Gibraltar and Africa; restaurants, bars, tennis and golf. 243 rooms.

Gran Meliá Don Pepe (5 stars GL) €€€€€ *José Meliá s/n, tel: 952 770 300, fax: 952 779 954, www.solmelia.es*. An imposing hotel just a 5-minute walk from the city centre. Only tropical gardens and pools separate it from the beach. Every expected luxury can be found here, plus a fitness centre and restaurants. 202 rooms.

NH Alanda (4 stars) €€€€ *Boulevar Principe Alfonso Von Hohenlohe S/N, tel: 952 899 600, fax: 952 764 846, www.nh-hotels.com*. Located west of Marbella, close to the mosque, this hotel, surrounded by its own tropical gardens, has large and attractive rooms, some specially adapted for the disabled. It also offers the Spa Elysium and sauna, and a poolside bar and restaurant. 196 rooms and 3 suites.

EL PUERTO DE SANTA MARÍA

Hotel Monasterio San Miguel (4 stars) €€€€–€€€€€ *Virgen de los Milagros 27, tel: 956 540 440, fax: 956 542 604, www.monasteriosanmiguelhotel.com.* An intriguing complex originally constructed in the 18th century as a Capuchin convent. The cells have been beautifully renovated. 165 rooms.

EL ROCÍO (COTO DOÑANA NATIONAL PARK)

El Cortijo de Los Mimbrales €€€€ *Carretera Rocío–Matalascañas, A483, Km30, tel: 959 442 237, fax: 959 442 443, www.cortijo mimbrales.com.* This is a beautiful manor house, in the heart of the Doñana National Park and close to the quaint village of El Rocío and the wide sandy beaches of Matalascañas. 36 rooms, 1 suite, 2 duplexes, 1 one-bedroom villa, 4 two-bedroom villas.

RONDA

Hotel Polo (3 stars) €€–€€€ *Mariano Soubirón 8, tel: 952 872 447, fax: 952 872 449, www.hotelpolo.net.* A hotel, right in the city centre, whose décor and atmosphere are a pleasing mix of the traditional and modern. The rooms are of a nice size and the hotel has its own impressive restaurant. 36 rooms.

SEVILLA

Casa Romana (4 stars) €€€€€ *Trajano 15, tel: 954 915 170, fax: 954 373 191, www.hotelcasaromana.com.* Close to the Sierpes pedestrian shopping street, this hotels has large, beautifully furnished rooms and public areas that include charming patios and the peaceful rooftop solarium. 26 rooms.

Hotel Husa Los Seises (4 stars) €€€€–€€€€€ *Segovias 6, tel: 954 229 495, fax: 954 224 334, www.hotellosseises.com.* A 16th-century palace blending historic surroundings with modern facilities to create an intriguing atmosphere. Central location in Barrio de Santa Cruz. Rooftop pool overlooking the Giralda. 42 rooms.

Hotel Maestranza (1 star) €€ *Gamazo 12, tel: 954 561 070, fax: 954 214 404, www.hotelmaestranza.es.* The Maestranza is located just off the Plaza Nueva, between the Cathedral and the Plaza de Toros, in an impressive mansion typical of Sevilla. 18 rooms.

La Casa del Maestro (1 star) €€€–€€€€ *Niño Ricardo 5, tel: 954 500 007, www.lacasadelmaestro.com.* This beautiful mansion, close to the Casa de Pilatos, was once the home of the guitarist Manuel Serrapi Sánchez and the décor here reflects his interests. The rooftop patio offers spectacular views of the La Giralda. 11 rooms.

Las Casas del Rey Baeza (5 stars) €€€€€ *Plaza Jesús de la Redención 2, tel: 954 561 496, fax: 954 561 441, www.hospes.es.* One of Sevilla's most prestigious hotels, with beautifully furnished rooms set around the courtyards. Rooftop pool and free use of bicycles. 36 rooms and 5 suites.

Petit Palace Marqués Santa Ana (4 stars) €€€–€€€€ *Jimios 9–11, tel: 954 221 812, fax: 954 228 993, www.sevillappmarquesantana. com.* The Marqués Santa Ana includes all the high-tech features that are a speciality of this interesting hotel chain. Located close to the Cathedral. 6 high-tech rooms, 33 double rooms and 18 family rooms.

TORREMOLINOS

Tropicana Hotel & Beach Club (4 stars) €€€ *Tropico 6, Box 29, tel: 952 386 600, fax: 952 380 568, www.hoteltropicana.net.* Situated right on La Carihuela beach, the Tropicana has an interesting character and is set in its own small garden with a pool, beach club and the prestigious Mango Restaurant. 84 rooms.

VILLANUEVA DE LA CONCEPCIÓN

La Posada del Torcal €€€€ *Villanueva de la Concepción, tel: 952 031 006, www.laposadadeltorcal.com.* A small, luxurious Andalusian farmhouse *(cortijo).* On an isolated hilltop, it has the rugged forms of El Torcal behind it and the Mediterranean in the distance below. Pool, spa and gourmet restaurant. 8 rooms.

Recommended Restaurants

The establishments recommended here are mostly traditional Andalusian restaurants serving local specialities (see 'Eating Out' section). The resorts along the coast are packed with cheaper (and blander) alternatives, ranging from fast-food outlets to Chinese, Indian and Italian restaurants.

Seafood restaurants line the waterfront in every town and are usually expensive – go inland for a block or two and the prices drop considerably, although the quality remains the same. Reservations are recommended for the more expensive places.

Lunch is generally served between 1.30 and 4pm and dinner between 9 and 11.30pm, although restaurants in the larger resorts tend to serve meals almost all day. As a basic guide to prices, we have used the following symbols to give some idea of the cost of lunch or dinner for two, not including drinks. All these restaurants accept the major credit cards unless otherwise noted.

€€€€€	over 60 euros
€€€€	35–60 euros
€	under 35 euros

BENALMÁDENA-COSTA

Mar de Alborán €€ *Avenida de Alay 5, tel: 952 446 427.* Near the marina in Benalmádena, this Basque-Andalusian restaurant specialises in good, fresh seafood. Closed Sunday evening and all day Monday.

CARMONA

Gracia Real €€€ *Plaza de Lasso 1, tel: 954 191 000.* The restaurant of the Casa de Carmona hotel *(see page 130)*, set in the wonderfully renovated stables of this former Renaissance palace. The exquisite furniture, silverware and crystal complement the classically prepared international and Andalusian dishes. Altogether, a delightful experience.

CÓRDOBA

Almudaina €€€ *Camposanto de los Mártires 1, tel: 957 474 342.* A carefully restored 16th-century palace. Distinguished surroundings enhance the traditional Córdoban cuisine, prepared with fresh market produce. Closed Sunday night.

El Churrasco €€€ *Romero 16, tel: 957 290 819.* Seasonal cuisine and wines from their own Wine Museum, served in a 14th-century house in the Jewish Quarter. Closed August.

ESTEPONA

Lido Restaurant €€€ *Las Dunas Hotel, La Boladilla Baja, Carretera de Cádiz, Km163.5, tel: 952 796 554.* Supreme service, Mediterranean cuisine from a Michelin-starred chef, piano music and sea views.

FUENGIROLA

La Caracola €€€ *Paseo Maritimo (Playa), tel: 952 584 687.* This restaurant on the beach has a relaxed atmosphere and serves specialities such as seafood casserole, small fried fish and fish baked in salt.

GRANADA

Chikito €€€ *Plaza del Campillo 9, tel: 958 223 364.* Typically Andalusian cuisine, a reasonably priced wine list and a city-centre location. Frequented by intellectuals and celebrities, whose photographs adorn the walls. Closed Wednesday.

La Yedra Real €–€€ *Paseo de la Sabika 15, tel: 958 229 145.* Located next to the Generalife gardens, this is a very pleasant modern restaurant with a nice terrace that offers typical Spanish dishes at very competitive prices. Open 9.30am–5pm, closed Monday.

Sevilla €€ *Oficios 12, tel: 958 221 223.* Granada's most famous restaurant was once a favourite of the poet Federico García Lorca.

The menu offers a good mix of local Granadino and Andalusian specialities. Closed Sunday evening.

JEREZ DE LA FRONTERA

El Bosque €€€ *Avenida Alcade Álvaro Domecq 26, tel: 956 307 303.* Prestigious restaurant serving traditional cuisine created with only the finest ingredients. Elegant dining rooms and a wine cellar of around 25,000 bottles. Closed Sunday and Monday evening

Tendido 6 €€€ *Circo 10, tel: 956 344 835.* Next to the Plaza de Toros, with bull-themed decor to match. Wide range of Andalusian cuisine and a mainly Spanish wine list.

EL MADROÑAL

Mesón El Coto €€–€€€ *Carretera de Ronda (7km/4 miles from San Pedro de Alcántara), tel: 952 786 688.* In the foothills of the Serranía de Ronda mountains and overlooking the coast, this lovely restaurant specialises in rabbit, partridge, quail, duck, wild boar, baby lamb and suckling pig, which you cook yourself on a red-hot stone.

MÁLAGA

Adolfo €€€ *Paseo Marítimo Pablo Ruiz Picasso 12, tel: 952 601 914.* Enjoy high-quality creative cooking with a menu that changes according to the season. Closed Sunday and three weeks in June.

Antigua Casa de Guardia € *Alameda Principal 18, tel: 952 214 680.* Founded in 1840 and hardly changed since. Huge wooden barrels of local wines, especially the sweet Málaga *dulce*, sit behind long wooden bars. Be sure to taste the small dishes of prawns, clams, mussels and other shellfish. Cash only. Closed Sunday.

Bar Orellana € *Moreno Monroy 5, tel: 952 223 012.* A small L-shaped bar and restaurant serving home-made Andalusian dishes and fabulous *tapas* that are popular with the locals, especially at weekends. Cash only. Closed Wed.

El Chinitas €€ *Moreno Monroy 4–6, tel: 952 210 972.* Restaurant in the Old Town specialising in Andalusian and Málagueño dishes. Eat in or on the pedestrianised street in front.

MARBELLA

La Pesquera del Faro €€€ *Playa del Faro, Paseo Maritimo, tel: 952 868 520.* A pleasant restaurant in the Pesquera chain. This one, on the beach, does great seafood and has a wonderful atmosphere.

EL PUERTO DE SANTA MARÍA

El Faro del Puerto €€–€€€ *Carretera de Rota, Km0.5, tel: 956 858 003, fax: 956 540 466.* Surrounded by its own gardens, this restaurant is renowned for creative cuisine with traditional dishes, and an extensive wine list. Closed Sunday night, except in August.

Romerijo €€€ *José Antonio Romero Zarazaga 1, tel: 956 541 254.* In a city famous for its seafood, this place, serving every variety of fish, is easily the most popular. Also does take-away.

SAN FERNANDO

Ventorrillo el Chato €€€ *Carretera Cádiz–San Fernando, Km687, tel: 956 250 225.* On the isthmus connecting Cádiz to San Fernando, this is a historic restaurant with an attractive Andalusian-style dining room. It has Andalusian-style cuisine, too, with tasty desserts and fine wines. Closed Sunday.

SEVILLA

Casa Robles €€€ *Alvarez Quintero 58, tel: 954 563 272.* This restaurant, in an 18th-century mansion close to the cathedral, is popular with locals and tourists alike. Does traditional Andalusian stews and seafood dishes along with home-made desserts.

Corral del Agua €€€ *Agua 6, tel: 954 224 841.* An attractive 17th-century house in the Barrio de Santa Cruz that serves classic Andalusian cuisine. Seating available on a lovely patio around a fountain. Closed Sunday.

Egaña Oriza €€€ *San Fernando 41, tel: 954 227 211, fax: 954 502 727.* Located in a beautiful building opposite the tobacco factory, Egaña Oriza is renowned for dishes that combine Basque influences with Andalusian traditions. Spanish and international wine list. Closed Sunday evening and August.

El Rinconcillo €€–€€€ *Gerona 40–42, tel: 954 223 183.* One of the oldest and most atmospheric *tapas* bars in the city, dating from the 17th century. A running account of your bill is chalked up on the wall.

Horacio €€€ *Antonio Díaz 9, tel: 954 225 385.* Situated close to the Plaza de Toros, the appealing Horacio has a creatively modern atmosphere, with Andalusian and international cuisine to match.

La Albahaca €€€ *Plaza Santa Cruz 12, tel: 954 220 714, fax: 954 561 204.* Housed in a typical Sevillana mansion, La Albahaca offers three dining rooms and alfresco dining in summer. Basque-based menu with exquisite seasonal dishes. Closed Sunday.

Los Seises €€€ *Segovias 6, tel: 954 229 495.* In the hotel of the same name, this restaurant, set around Roman and Moorish excavations, offers top regional cuisine and desserts with Arabic influences.

Río Grande €€€ *Betis s/n, tel: 954 273 956.* This is a fine restaurant in its own right, and offers a tempting array of typically Spanish cuisine. But, located just across the San Telmo bridge, its huge picture windows also offer the finest views of the Torre de Oro and La Giralda in all Sevilla.

TORREMOLINOS

Frutos €€ *Avenida de la Riviera 80, tel: 952 381 450, fax: 952 371 377.* Reputed to be Torremolinos' best restaurant with an enclosed terrace and air-conditioning throughout. The cuisine is a meeting of Castilian grilled meats and Andalux fish and seafood.

INDEX

Berlitz pocket guide

Costa del Sol & Andalucía

Thirteenth Edition 2010
Reprinted 2012

Written by Norman Renouf
Updated by Nick Inman and Clara Villanueva
Series Editor: Tom Stainer

Photography credits
AGE Fotostock 23; Chris Coe 19, 24, 30, 32,
39, 59, 99; Jerry Dennis 8, 9, 14, 16, 31, 37, 45,
50, 51, 84, 89, 95; istockphoto 6, 10, 18, 26, 29,
36, 40, 41, 42, 46, 48, 53, 55, 57, 58, 62, 64, 66,
71, 72, 78, 81, 82, 88, 92, 100, 102; Mark Read
11, 13, 17, 21, 35, 44, 69, 74, 77, 80, 85, 91;
Gregory Wrona 87, 96, 101; Real Escuela
Andaluza del Arte Ecuestre 60; NHPA 61

Cover picture: 4CornersImages